THE WORLD OF CRUISING

*A series of uniform paperback editions
reprinting some of the most popular and
readable narratives from the world of
the cruising – and racing – sailor, past
and present.*

Also by Adlard Coles

Heavy Weather Sailing
North Biscay Pilot
Channel Harbours & Anchorages
North Brittany Harbours & Anchorages
Shell Pilot to the South Coast Harbours
North Atlantic
Close-Hauled
In Broken Waters*
In Finnish Waters*
Mary Anne Among 10,000 Islands*
Sailing Days*
Sailing and Cruising*
Yacht Racing Rules Simplified*

*These titles are not in print at present

CLOSE HAULED

BEING THE ADVENTURES OF THE AUTHOR & HIS WIFE CRUISING
ALONE, IN A 29-FOOT KETCH, AMONGST THE LESSER
KNOWN ISLANDS OF THE BALTIC DURING A
VOYAGE FROM LATVIA TO ENGLAND

BY

K. ADLARD COLES, F.R.G.S.

AUTHOR OF "IN BROKEN WATER"

ILLUSTRATED BY

H. ALKER TRIPP ("LEIGH HOE")

NAUTICAL

© K Adlard Coles Estate 1926

First published in Great Britain in 1926 by
Seeley, Service & Co. Ltd.

First published in paperback in Great Britain 1987 by
Nautical Books
An imprint of Conway Maritime Press Ltd
24 Bride Lane, Fleet Street
London EC4Y 8DR

ISBN 0 85177 420 2

Printed in Great Britain by Oxford University Press

PREFACE

JUST as one cruise leads to another so a first book leads to a second; and the writer has been encouraged to recount a further experience of long-distance sailing in the present volume, *Close Hauled*.

The two cruises were, however, very different in nature, for the object of the first in taking a six-ton yacht to Copenhagen and back was to find adventure, whereas the attractions of the second lay in the exploring of places, islands and fiords out of the tourists' tracks, and in the meetings with fishermen, sailors and other followers of the sea. That was the purpose in this cruise from Riga, but an element of adventure also existed ; for the voyage had to be started very late in the season, and the prevailing contrary winds often forced *Annette II* to thrash her way close hauled against heavy head seas, straining the strength of her light crew of two (the writer and his wife) to the uttermost.

In the present book, as in the former, no endeavour has been made to gull the reader into awestruck—or shall we say borestruck ?—admiration of nautical phraseology. Nor has any attempt been made to adopt a definite method of treating the subject. The writer has taken things just as they came, winds and calms, rocks and shoals, ships and harbours, people and countries. In this short cruise it is claimed that there has been almost as much variety as in

7

PREFACE

a cruise round the world for, not only was there navigation in narrow seas, but there were coastal passages and deep sea voyages from one country to another, taking as much as three days at a time.

It is possible that the narrative conveys an impression of too much hardship, but, whatever the difficulties, the cruise is looked back on as a happy holiday ; and it is hoped that the book will in some measure reflect the atmosphere of utter freedom, with its troubles and humours, that made the voyage in foreign waters so attractive to the " skipper " and the " crew."

The writer wishes to thank the original owner of *Annette II* for passing on to him such a seaworthy ship ; and to thank Mr. Alker Tripp for describing by brush much that the author could not convey in writing.

K. A. C.

HUNDESTED HARBOUR

CONTENTS

THE MOLE AT YMUIDEN

Introduction

Surely one of the best loved of all yachting authors, Adlard
Coles was a pioneer of the art of family cruising in small craft,
besides being a guide to yachting pilotage in many waters.

The delightfully modest description of adventures when he,
aged 24, and his young wife, sailed a 29-foot boat from Latvia to
England, makes his book *Close-Hauled* a classic. It was first
published exactly sixty years ago, and as Latvia is now part of
the Soviet Union, that part of the cruise is generally no longer
visited by yachtsmen.

The book had an intriguing secret that was not disclosed for
thirty years. The yacht, re-named *Annette II*, was actually the
already famous *Racundra* which Arthur Ransome sold for 200
guineas on condition that Adlard Coles would not mention her
original name in the book which was to become *Close-Hauled*.
Perhaps this was to avoid confusion with Ransome's own book
Racundra's First Cruise. The sale was a good bargain for Adlard
Coles, as it led him on to a whole lifetime of venturesome
cruising, but perhaps a bad bargain for Arthur Ransome, whose
health deteriorated when he gave up the sea. The boat herself
was still sailing in the 1970s, but I believe she was then lost in the
West Indies.

Close-Hauled was written for whoever finds interest in
adventure, out of the way places and the sea in general. It tells
with special charm how a foreign, family cruise creates an
atmosphere of utter freedom, with all its troubles and humour.
This was the second of his sailing books of which he wrote
many over a period of some sixty years.

Adlard Coles became a renowned ocean racing skipper, being
elected Yachtsman of the Year in 1957 for his achievement in this
aspect of sailing. However, it was as a cruising man that he was
awarded the Gold Medal of the Royal Institute of Navigation
while, for his services to yachting generally, he was honoured
with the OBE. His deep knowledge of boats and sailing,
combined with his natural modesty, made him well loved as well
as respected.

Erroll Bruce
1987

A DANISH HARBOUR

LIST OF ILLUSTRATIONS IN TEXT

DUTCH TORPEDO BOAT

13

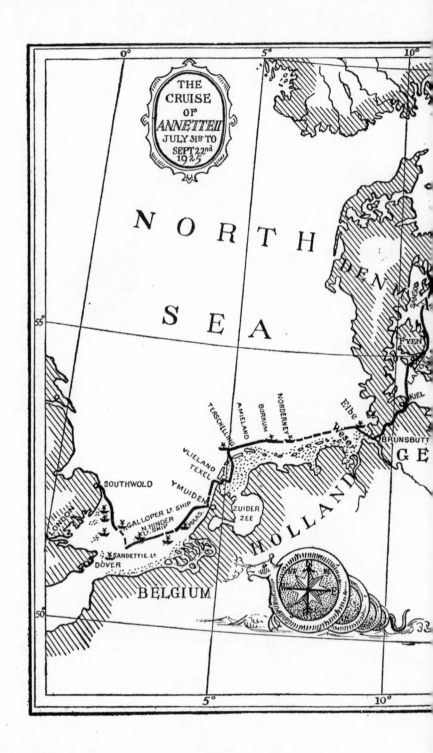

LONGEST INDIVIDUAL SAILS

	SEA MILES SAILED	SEA MILES DIRECT	HOURS
(a). Dome Ness (Latvia) to Ljugarn (Gotland)........	160	140	49
(b). Sles Viken (Gotland) to Karlskrona (Sweden)......	140	130	50
(c). Skillinge (Sweden) to Copenhagen (Denmark).....	70	70	80
(d). Brunsbuttel (Germany) to Vlieland (Holland)...	180	170	60
(e). Ymuiden (Holland) to Southwold (England)......	175	105	53

DAY SAILING ~~~~~
NIGHT SAILING ─ ─ ─ ─

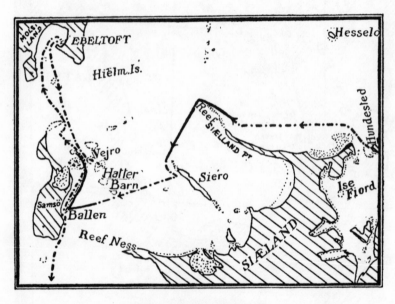

AMONG THE DANISH ISLANDS

Hundested to Ballen, including a night at sea lost in a rain squall, when the yacht and her crew drifted by chance through the narrow rock-strewn sound between Samsö and Vejrö, finding themselves at dawn twenty miles north of their course.

Day sailing shown by dotted line. *Night sailing* in full line.

See pp. 100–118.

CHAPTER I

A LINE of white dust and a succession of sneezes marked the progress of a cyclist along the Portsmouth Road, on a blazing evening when the whole countryside was glowing under the unexpected enthusiasm of a fine June. It was the kind of weather in which poets find inspiration and business men find infuriation. In short, it was too hot, and the cyclist found it almost intolerable. The ravages of heat, hay fever and dust combined to make things so unpleasant that the mind of the rider left the scorching road, with its incessant stream of noisy motors, to picture visions of cool seas and wind-swept islands.

As it happened, these dreams were to materialise through an advertisement of a yacht for sale at a distant port—but before going further the cyclist must be introduced. He was the writer of this book.

On the same day that I heard of the offer I wrote for full particulars, as such an opportunity was not to be missed through delay in making the necessary enquiries. The yacht was lying some thousand miles away, offering a chance of a most delightful cruise in foreign waters; and the price, moreover, was within the means of a person poor enough not to despise the pedals of a second-hand " grid " as a means of locomotion. There were many other reasons why this advertisement held my fancy. The yacht was almost new, was well known even in England as a powerful sea boat, and, above all, could be managed by a slight crew consisting merely of the owner and his wife.

No reply came to my letter, and I started making enquiries in Denmark and Sweden for other craft that might be suitable. Answers to these enquiries arrived in course of time, but there appeared to be few yachts for sale that would have been of use, and those that might have done seemed very highly valued. The long cruise looked as though destined to be a voyage pencilled on the charts that had already been purchased in its anticipation; but at length one day early in July an envelope arrived armed with a stamp that immediately drew attention. It was from Latvia apologising for the delay in answering, and explaining that my letter had been forwarded from an old address. What was more important, it contained the particulars required; and my wife decided we should buy, which, I may add, settled the matter once and for all.

Final negotiations took up a considerable time, as the owner was returning to England and had no definite address; but the day arrived at last when we could see the way to book a cabin on a steamer bound to Riga on July 16th, and we calculated on being able to sail on our own ship by the 1st of August. Even this date was a very late one for starting in the Baltic; as the best time of the year there is spring, when the days are long and fair winds from the East are frequent.

At last Wednesday, the day of departure, really arrived; and in the evening our taxi picked its way amongst the queer collection of humanity that throng the streets in the vicinity of the London docks. The taxi moved slowly, but it had not far to go from Waterloo before it turned away from busy thoroughfares into a side street, then through an arch and, finally, with quick turn to the right, it came to a standstill in front of another arch.

As that presumably was Hay's Wharf I got out and walked over to ask the name of the nearest ship, which proved to be the *Kolpino*—the Wilson liner that was to take us across the North Sea and along the Baltic coast to Riga, where our true adventure was to start. I returned to the taxi with a steward to collect the boxes, and in a very short time we were in our cabin unpacking such luggage as we thought might be necessary. The weather had been intensely hot and it was like an oven below—so hot that the value of a bathe in clean sparkling water would have been above mere money. It was tiring to stand up and wearying to lie down.

The *Kolpino* was a ship of three or four thousand tons, which ran a more or less coastal service from London or Hull to the ports of the southern Baltic. Her primary consideration was probably cargo ; but she also had accommodation for second-class passengers, and quite nice quarters for the saloon class, in a deck house that had been built on the ship some years after she had been launched.

On this particular run her chief cargo consisted of some Polish cavalry that had been doing great things at Olympia. The horses, two dozen in number, were placed in stalls on each side of the hold on the foredeck. They seemed very docile animals, and submitted without any signs of interest to being lifted, together with their boxes, by a crane right up into the air before being gently lowered to the deck.

THE ADVENTURE BEGINS

The ship was due to start at 8 p.m., but some of the cargo was late in arriving, so that we had to wait in the sweltering heat until close on midnight. Part of the time was occupied in having dinner, when we took the opportunity of observing our fellow-passengers. They were an odd selection indeed. First of all we noticed the " Baron," a slim man aged between twenty-six and forty-six, whom we learnt was a Russian who had lost most of his possessions in the revolution, and was now in the diplomatic service of some comparatively obscure nation. He had lived in Riga and was one of the fortunate few who had benefited through the recent arrangement between the Latvian and the Soviet Governments, by which he recovered all his jewels which had been stolen during the revolution.

Another passenger bound for Riga was a stout little man with long hair, bushy eyebrows and moustaches, who was believed to be a manufacturer. His sister had been murdered in the revolution.

Then there was the Polish officer who lacked the arrogance so common to foreign army men ; and also a mixture of foreigners of various nationalities. Amongst these the large fat figure of a padré always stood out conspicuously amongst the lesser brethren. He was rather an unpleasant-looking fellow, and we found out later that he had come on board under somewhat peculiar circumstances. He had sent literally half a ton of luggage to the ship, but when he arrived in person he tendered a pound note instead of his fare of twelve guineas. He insisted on seeing the captain and told him that a certain great steamship company had taken him from America at a special price. The captain was a Yorkshireman and did not appear to have much sympathy for the Roman Church, for after a short discussion he ordered the luggage to be put back on the wharf. Thereupon the padré held a collection amongst the Poles for his passage money ; and secured not only sufficient for his first-class fare, but also for plenty of wine on the voyage. He had been to America to raise money and clothes for his little flock in Lithuania. A most excellent object no doubt; but one would have thought more of it, were it not for the fact that it involved a first-class passage to America and back, with every luxury for the collector.

Another interesting person was a man with a podgy white face of the perspiring type, who spoke American with a strong German accent. He had not been in Europe for some years, but he was returning now full of " ideals." He was an avowed Bolshevik, but appeared quite well-to-do and, like all reformers, he managed to travel in great personal comfort.

Towards midnight a sudden blast from the tug alongside momentarily petrified us with its shrill violence. Warps were cast off and the *Kolpino* was gradually pushed, pulled and cursed into mid-stream, and her voyage begun. Astern London Bridge threw its bright lighted span across the river ; and on each side the flares on the wharves were reflected in the water, which was thrashed into a fury of little wavelets by the tugs with barges that passed up and down in constant stream. On the northern side of the Thames a dark broken line against the sky outlined the shapes of the buildings. These were slipping by ; the shadowed silhouette of the Tower Bridge embraced us ; and the ship passed out along the lines of docks down the dark river.

A fresh breeze was blowing into our cabin through the open porthole, so that sleep came naturally instead of having to be won against the resisting forces of heat, almost tropical in fierceness ; but rest for the weary was not to last long, as, after two short hours, sounds of feverish activity broke the silence of the night.

The engines had stopped and the pilot was engaged in a somewhat lurid conversation with a hand on the forecastle. It appeared that he wanted to anchor, but the windlass had jammed. The ebb tide meanwhile was sweeping the ship along in great style amongst other vessels at anchor, until the pilot in a state of considerable agitation rang the engines astern. The *Kolpino* is designed to go forward, and when this is happening her machinery cannot be felt, but as soon as she is required to go astern the poor lady shakes with rage, and her engines raise a tremendous din. Presently, however, the anchor dropped and all was well again.

At breakfast next morning we learnt that some cargo had been forgotten and had been sent after us. It appeared that this unusual event had filled some of the Polish ladies with consternation, and that they had rushed on deck attired as they were in nightdresses and ear-rings. They thought the ship was sinking and refused to return to their cabins. It must have been rather chilly for them, as they remained there until daylight dispelled their fears.

The passage across the North Sea was eventless, and we were glad when on Friday morning land appeared. It was the German coast near the entrance to the River Elbe ; and at about midday the *Kolpino* entered the Brunsbüttel locks, which cut off the Kiel Canal from the North Sea. Two hours were spent there in coaling which was effected by a large mechanical stoker. A steel framework on which ran a little trolley was lowered from the shore over the ship. From this trolley a huge scoop was suspended which alternatively took up coal from the shore, ran out along the framework, and dropped it into a canvas funnel leading to the bunkers.

There were two of these mechanical arrangements at Brunsbüttel, and but two weeks previous to our arrival one of them had toppled over on the ship it was coaling. The vessel was sunk, but I was told that, although indignation waxed high, there were no casualties.

At dusk we were still in the Kiel Canal, for it takes about six hours to pass through. The occasion was interesting to me, as the last time that I had been through I had seen the place from the cockpit of a six-ton yacht, which is very different in perspective ; but, even when viewed from the high decks of a great steamer, there is nothing on the canal to arouse any enthusiasm. It cuts a curving path through flat agricultural country, and is lined by stone banks with white painted marks at even distances apart. The most striking features are the high bridges that cross the water at a great height in order to allow the masts of large steamers to pass below. One of these is for a railway ; and we watched a diminutive train slowly ascend the long gradient that leads to the bridge and then cross high in the air, where it looked like a toy, and finally swing down the great curve that brought it down to the level of the land once more. German structures are remarkable for their lightness. Everything we passed seemed built with a view to saving every ounce of steel.

Steamship voyages are the same the world over, and ours was no exception. Time was passed in eating, sleeping and talking to fellow-passengers. Our first call was at Danzig, where the Polish horses were landed, together with most of the passengers. As there was a considerable amount of cargo to be discharged there was time for passengers to go ashore. We went under the guidance of a small boy named " Isaak," who not only acted as interpreter but took charge of the party. He was only about nine years old and was returning to Riga for his holidays from an English school, but he was one of those boys that make one feel very young and flippant. When we said anything he would turn his head, which was adorned with a large mop of most brilliant red hair, and listen to find out whether there was anything on which he could advise or explain. We got into a train that runs from the harbour to the town and then separated there from the rest of the party to explore on our own. Quite by accident we happened on an immensely high red building set in the heart of the town, and so closely surrounded by houses that it was impossible to be seen properly. It appeared to rise out of these like a monster growth : uncouth, unkempt. Without any great effort we guessed it was what in Poland corresponded to a cathedral, and afterwards learnt it was over five hundred years old ; but of its history all we could find out was that it had been used by Napoleon as a hospital and stables.

We had a cup of coffee sitting outside a café overlooking the Square, and watched the people as they passed. The women dress most remarkably badly, and their clothes are worn like sacks put on as an afterthought. Danzig was at that time in a period of transition when stately matrons strutted along in short skirts, whilst comparatively slender but less up-to-date maidens were still to be seen in the long garments peculiar to 1924. Most nationalities seemed to be represented in Danzig, but whatever the nationality they all had one characteristic in common—fat !

Having met the rest of our party for lunch we went back to the *Kolpino*, which left the docks early in the afternoon.

At about nine next morning sounds of music dispelled sleep, and shortly afterwards a shouting together with a certain amount of language betrayed the fact that the ship was bringing up in a port. I knew it must be Memel and so went to sleep again. At breakfast the ship was again at sea ; but when we heard the story of the music we really regretted not having got up to see what had been happening. It appeared that it had been a welcome to the padré on his return to his country. There were two brass bands that first played a tune together, and afterwards started a competition on their own to show what they could effect individually. The result was hardly pleasing to the ear, but of enthusiasm there was no doubt. The mayor, assisted by two of his council, met the padré when he landed and embraced him, kissing him on both cheeks. The picture must have been most moving, but the captain was in no mood to appreciate it, for he was in a hurry, and on the quay were neither agents, nor Customs officials nor dockers. He sent a boy for the agent, but the boy failed to return. All the time the bands played, feverishly endeavouring to drown each other's noise. The captain's temper was sore tried, but after some delay he got the cargo discharged.

The same morning the *Kolpino* touched at Libau, where there is an immense harbour composed of huge blocks of stone thrown roughly down to make the moles. At the end of one of these lies the wreck of a Russian cruiser which, after the war, was sold to Germany for scrap iron. On the way to Germany she fell in with very bad weather and was driven up on to the mole, where she still rests. The funnels and masts are still intact and the hull does not appear to be much damaged ; which is surprising in view of the fact that every gale must sweep over the vessel.

Libau, like many of these Baltic ports, has a history. It was designed as a premier naval port by Alexander of Russia, but was abandoned in the ensuing reign of Nicholas as it was thought to be too near Germany for safety. The base for the fleet was then removed to the Black Sea.

We waited in the harbour for some time until, shortly before lunch, a tug came off to the ship, and quite a crowd climbed aboard. Two of these were passengers and the remainder included friends, Customs officials, and a Bolshevik agent. Most of these were in uniforms of variegated design, but the Russian merely wore a straw hat as an emblem of authority.

As soon as the friends could be induced to return to the tug the *Kolpino* steamed out.

THE TRADE ROUTE

CHAPTER II

RIGA—THE PETERSBURG—DROSHKIES—DVINA SALMON—
KAISERWALD—"ANNETTE II"—LETT, RUSSIAN AND BALT
—PUSSYFOOT IN LATVIA

AFTER a voyage of five days the ship entered Riga on July 22nd ; and from 6 a.m. a continuous hubbub kept us awake. We had arranged the previous night to have breakfast at 7.30, but at half-past six there was a knock on the cabin door and the stewardess announced that passports must be shown and luggage put ashore. In answer to my enquiry why they disturbed us so early, she replied that there was an hour's extra summer time in Latvia ; and added, as an afterthought, that it was an "heathen" country. The stewardess, I may add, was Swedish.

It was annoying to have to wash, dress and pack at five minutes' notice, but the prospect of being ashore at Riga smoothed our injured feelings. We had breakfast and bade a hurried good-bye to the friends made during the passage ; and we succeeded in arriving at the Customs house shortly after 8 a.m. The examination of our luggage was more formal than thorough, so that it was not long before we were lodged in a "taximeter," with luggage piled high over our legs.

Riga is one of the most attractive towns in Northern Europe, and its fascination made itself felt the moment we left the Customs house. Everything was so fundamentally

27

foreign. The taximeter dashed along on the right hand side of the cobbled streets, passing Russian houses which have narrow square openings that do justice for windows. We met few motor cars, for the national vehicle is the "droshky"—a one-horse carriage of close relationship to bath chairs and hansoms—driven by ruffians wearing a kind of uniform consisting mainly of a blue coat and a black leather hat.

The taximeter drew up in front of the Petersburg Hotel, where we were met by the head porter—a man of such striking appearance that we labelled him unhesitatingly "the Archduke." He took us up to the floor above and showed us a magnificent suite of rooms ; but, finding these secured more admiration than financial interest, he beckoned us up another flight of stairs, and offered a slightly smaller set of rooms at the price of twelve lats a day. These were cheap enough, but as we should be on the yacht during the day we asked whether he had not simply a large room. The Archduke was disappointed, but passive, and conducted us to the second floor where we were shown a very nice room at six lats a day. Now, as twenty-five lats correspond to an English pound, this sum amounted roughly to five shillings—half a crown each per day. We accepted !

The hotel is the best in Riga. It is old fashioned, and was built when the Balt Germans were the greatest power in the city. The rooms are very high and the furniture massive. Even the doors are of flat solid timber, closed by great hand-made keys that clatter in the locks and echo down the dark passages that run from end to end of the building. Large fire-places enclosed in brick, looking like miniature furnaces, are built up in each room ; and they reminded us that Riga is under snow for the greater part of the year.

Below our window was a cobbled street where one or two droshkies were usually to be found waiting a casual fare ; then an open space with a few trees ; and facing us was the "Schloss"—a large cream-coloured building. This, we afterwards learnt, was built by a semi-religious, semi-adventurous order of German colonists in the year 1230 ; but was in later years captured and rebuilt by the Swedes.

We went down for coffee and rolls. The dining-room was a long low room decorated in blue and having walnut furniture of a high, ornate design. The waiter was delighted to serve English people and, although his knowledge of our language was limited, his willingness to help was immeasurable. Whenever he brought anything he bowed and said, " pleeze," a word employed also when he took away a plate or was asked for bread. In fact, even if the time was asked, the answer was " pleeze ! " His great feat, however, he accomplished on the second day of our stay at Riga, when he persuaded us to have salmon which he insisted was " ver goot." Very good it was too : fresh caught in the Dvina, then boiled, and afterwards fried. It imparted a most inviting smell as the knife cut through the bright bread crumbs and exposed the delicate pink colour of the fish itself.

Our first duty at Riga was to get some Latvian money at the bank, an operation both tiring and annoying, for the atmosphere of banks tends to dignity rather than speed. There are two currencies in Latvia—roubles and lats. Fifty roubles equal 1 lat and twenty-five lats approximate to an English pound. The reader, if he be energetic, will thus calculate that 100 roubles equals 2 lats, and an easy method of cheating is apparent. A price may be agreed upon, say 1·25, but when it comes to pay the discovery is made that the figure means 125 roubles, not 1 lat 25 cent-times. We made this discovery many times.

It was the yacht that had drawn us all those hundreds of miles from our home, so clearly that must be our first consideration. Hailing a droshky we explained to its driver that he was to take us to the Sportsverein Kaiserwald. Not only did this require some moments to penetrate his thick skull, but afterwards it took him a remarkable time to find his way in his own city. Many were the corners he turned, many the streets, and in fact many the well-ordered avenues of the Kaiserwald, until at last, after numerous enquiries of passers-by, he stopped in front of a gate over which a large notice showed that we had arrived at our destination. We left him and walked down towards a streak of blue that we knew must be the Stintsee. This requires some explanation. The Stintsee is practically a lake to the north of Riga—yet not quite a lake, as a narrow channel called the Muhlgraben connects it with the River Dvina. On the south of this water nearest the town lies the Kaiserwald, an extensive park, split up by wide shady avenues and large private houses standing back in their own grounds. Near the lake fields run down to the water which is hemmed by reeds. In a little " Stintsee " of diminutive proportions leading out of the main lake lived one by name Captain Sehmel, and it was to him that we bore a letter of introduction from the old owner of the yacht that we had re-named *Annette II*. He it was who had charge of the ship that was so soon to be ours. He had looked after her from the moment her stem first touched the water ; and she was in spirit as much his ship as she was her old owner's ; for it was he who had dressed her in paint, oiled her decks, rigged her gear, and shared her every cruise.

After many enquiries addressed in English to persons who had no knowledge of languages other than Lettish and German we found our way to Sehmel's abode by his little harbour. His wife was there, and managed to explain that he was due back in the evening. She then called to a passer-by, thereby finding by pure luck an interpreter. He was a young German, clad in flannels and flourishing a tennis racquet. English he spoke perfectly, and he soon made an appointment for me to meet Sehmel the following morning. He was extremely obliging, and insisted on giving up his game to show us the way to the Riga Yacht Club, which stood a few hundred yards away. In the shed belonging to the club lay *Annette* ; and it was with considerable excitement that we hurried forward to the first introduction to our ship.

From preliminary descriptions she was quite unmistakable : bluff-bowed, beamy, strong-looking, with the fine pointed stern that I have always admired in Scandinavian ships. A ladder was brought and we climbed up to her deck. Here the beam of nearly twelve feet looked very conspicuous but not unpleasing ; for the lines, guided by a good designer, were true. Over the companion a heavy oak top was latched down, but this could readily be opened and folded back. Down a few steps we went, past large cupboards and lockers, then through a diminutive opening into the cabin. Cabin, perhaps, is not the right word ; for the pride of *Annette* should rather be termed a room. It is huge for a twelve-ton yacht ; it is even large for a twenty-ton yacht, being about ten feet long, about eight wide and full six high. It is possible to walk about, to stretch one's arms, to dress, to think without any restraint. On each side lie wide bunks, backed by ample lockers. A table occupies the centre, and in one corner is a desk large enough for a full-sized chart. Forward, a door leads to the forecastle, where the anchor chains and spare sails are stored ; it also contains cupboards for small gear and one narrow bunk.

Of course, to describe feelings on introduction to a ship that has since passed into one's own hands is not easy. This was to be the ship to carry us through storm and calm, rain and sunshine. The ship to be looked after, the ship to look after us ; to whose strong timbers our lives were to be trusted. She was a real ship, too; for just as the *Berengaria* or some other great liner could cleave her way across the Atlantic, so, too, could the new *Annette* thrash her way through wild weather, or lie safely hove-to in a heavy gale. Many readers will not understand that a thirty-foot yacht is a real ship, sufficient in size to cross oceans ; they will not realise that a six-tonner is also a ship that can face a bad hammering, that can ride the sea when even large steamers are having an anxious time. Indeed, many sailing men do not know the power in their own yachts, for a well-designed yacht can be as safe as a lifeboat. From this let it not be imagined that the writer intended to put *Annette* to the test. Far from it, for bad weather is hell on a small ship and to be avoided where possible ; but it was pleasant to know that it was a safe hell that could, if necessary, be endured.

From this it will be gathered that *Annette* was not only a fine sea boat but in no way an ordinary vessel ; and these impressions are quite correct. She had many good points besides many faults ; but she was not ordinary. A fuller description of her virtues and vices is given in the Appendix.

Just as the steamer passage had proved longer than anticipated, so our visit to Riga proved proportionately shorter.
We saw Captain Sehmel the next day and he at once started
preparing *Annette* for sea. He was a little old man, fragile
in appearance, strong in fact. In his time he had served in
British ships and his career at sea had been very varied.
Not many years ago he had accumulated savings to buy
a clipper, or a share in a clipper—I forget which. He ran
this successfully for some years ; but on one unlucky
Saturday he telegraphed to the agents to insure his ship,
and he sailed without waiting for an acknowledgment.
On Sunday his ship was sunk, and he wired that she was
lost. On Monday he learnt that his first telegram had not
arrived in time, and that both had come together—so he
received no compensation, and returned to Riga to look
after little yachts and boats. He was an able rigger, very
attached to *Annette*, very loyal to *Annette's* old owner, and
very honest with us. The members of the yacht club did
not seem to share our high opinion of him, but we noticed
that they did not treat him with any great civility, and he
on his part failed to feign much respect for them. To us,
however, he was everything to be desired; and when we
sailed he even refused the amount I offered him beyond his
very moderate charges for fitting out.

Thus much time was on our hands ; and we were able
to see a lot of the city of Riga, although, as we were unable
to speak Lettish or German, we did not find out as much
of its history and position as we should have liked. There
is a charm about the place and the people that is definite
yet subtle. A sort of Orientalism that is yet not Eastern.
The cobbled streets, the droshkies, the houses, the peasants,
breathe an air of romance—and we knew that romance

existed there, waiting only to be found ; for Riga is a very old city, and has seen many nations and many wars. From the narrow main streets the traveller will suddenly turn into even narrower side streets where old, almost decaying houses face each other. There is a smell about the whole place, strange, not unpleasant, and peculiar to Riga.

In Latvia there are three powers that count : the Balt German who made Riga and the wealth of the place ; the Lett, the native of the country, who took advantage of the Treaty of Versailles to declare his independence ; and lastly the Russian. The latter of course is not in obvious evidence, but his influence is there, and his army is only over a nominal boundary. The feeling between the Balts and the Letts is at the moment very hostile. The Balts have for centuries been the ruling class, and now that the comparatively ignorant Letts are top dogs, the latter are intent on settling old grievances by the over-exertion of their new authority. Thus Riga is not only cosmopolitan, but it is also a town whose future is uncertain. Latvia is at present living on capital—selling timber without planting new trees. Russia is also in a condition even more uncertain, for it is said that the peasants are getting restless as they want many things which, if manufactured by their own countrymen, are too expensive to buy ; and which cannot be bought from abroad without causing annoyance to the industrial workers. Russia is said to be encouraging art to keep her people from thinking too much, but the last card is likely to be war, and Latvia will be the first involved. Unfortunately for Russia the Letts make good soldiers.

The cost of living in Riga is low, although heavy import duties are levied on such products as tinned goods and silk. Food is excellent, but on the rich side; and the restaurants are inexpensive. M——, a friend we had made on the steamer, once asked us out to dinner, where we partook of one of the national dishes. Layer after layer of rich foods were piled on top of each other, like some monstrous wedding cake. Salmon was there, cheese, crayfish, sardines, besides many so-called dainties which we did not care to analyse. It was, however, another evening when we were dining together, that we learnt a little of the law in Latvia. We were in the middle of the meal when a waiter dashed up and made what was clearly an attempt to remove our beer. This we indignantly refused to allow, and the fellow departed in a state of great agitation. The cause of this trouble suddenly appeared. A little man of savage demeanour slowly strode across the restaurant glaring in every direction, and wherever he looked a hush ensued. He passed our table and then disappeared, leaving no doubt as to his identity. Clearly alcohol in any shape or form was not to be drunk in public after ten o'clock. We afterwards found that even beer was unprocurable from midday Saturday until Monday morning. Fortunately this discovery was made in time for us to be prepared. Moreover, the usual forms of evasion exist, and beer can be served up in coffee-pots.

The weather was intensely, tropically hot. All day and every day a vague thirst never left us, and every movement was an effort. It was just our luck to have this heat wave when most busy. Fitting out a ship for sea is anything but a holiday. The things to be attended to were numberless, and we used to welcome the evenings when, after the heat of the day, we were free to sit down in the cool and listen to the music in the gardens. Music, and good music at that, is very popular in Riga.

Thus time passed and *Annette* was launched ; her masts stepped ; and she was towed round to the little harbour where she lay close under the loving care of Sehmel. Every afternoon we took one of the motor buses that have lately appeared in Riga, and drove out to the Stintsee to see what progress was being made with the fitting out ; and we found that Sehmel was doing wonders.

Annette had a motor, a 5-h.p. Skandia, which filled me with no little misgiving, for I did not understand internal combustion engines. What was more, I had seen this one bodily under water just after *Annette* had been launched, and a dim suspicion crossed my mind that these smelly monsters were fed with oil, not with water. However, Sehmel assured me that it would take no harm and, as the planks of the ship " took up " in twenty-four hours, I forgot the matter—for a time!

Provisioning.—We had taken some provisions out with us by steamer from Messrs. Browns' Stores, Southampton, but we had not taken very much, fearing trouble with the Customs. As it turned out our fears were groundless for the stores passed into Latvia free of duty, and we greatly regretted not having brought more since part of our slender supply was stolen at Danzig. Moreover we found tinned goods very expensive abroad, and of somewhat inferior quality. In fact it would be no exaggeration to say that in 1925 the cost of food was lower in England than in any of the countries we visited. In Sweden prices were extremely high, biscuits, for example, costing five shillings a pound.

Thus the stores we had brought from England (consisting of two large bottles of Horlick's Malted Milk, a few tins of baked beans and soups, and a large tin of ships biscuits), came to be highly prized. We saved these for the not infrequent occasions when cooking was impossible, or so difficult as to make it not worth while.

A SAILING BREEZE

CHAPTER III

FINAL PREPARATIONS—THE START—GHOSTS OF THE PAST—
DVINA RIVER—DEVIATION—COASTING THE GULF OF
RIGA—DOME NESS—A PERFECT DAY—VODKA

THINGS were almost ready, and our last day at the hotel had arrived. We spent the morning provisioning at a small shop where negotiations were carried on in a mixture of English, German, French and Lettish. After this we bade farewell to the hotel, and started out for the Sportsverein in a taxi which positively bulged with the pile of luggage and stores. The ship's gear had been sent down the previous day in a cart, under the supervision of three messengers of the Riga Express Company. They looked rather a picturesque set of villains, and, were it not that I had been informed of their complete honesty, I should have felt anxious as to the safety of the luggage entrusted to their hands. They wore hats of semi-military appearance, and loose blue shirts tied round their waists by a length of rope which also served the purpose of making secure the large black wallets in which the messages were put. The first day we were in Riga we had noticed these men loafing about the street corners, but we then had laboured under the erroneous impression that they were hangmen off duty.

All the time since we had left England the weather had been tropically hot, but, now that comfort was left behind, the first spots of rain fell, and no sooner than we were on the ship than a deluge started. *Annette* had been laid up in a shed during the winter, so that her seams offered little opposition to the elements. The water trickled through in gentle streams as we unpacked and, but for the size of the cabin, it would have been a miserable business. As it was we were able to choose dry corners.

Thus we spent the first hours on our new ship, and when dusk came we lit the table lamp and the cabin seemed warm and cheerful. To save washing up we had dinner at the Riga Yacht Club, at the same time paying the bill for the launching of *Annette*. The members had been very pessimistic about my chances of getting away from Latvia with only the British papers. They said they were of no use in Latvia, and that I should have to become a member of their club to get proper papers ; and to become a member of their club I should have to wait two weeks for election. Some members were exceedingly good to us, but I fancy others were offended with the idea of our managing without their assistance.

Next morning we went back to the city and met a young man at the hotel who was to act as interpreter, and set off in a droshky for the offices of the Marine Department. Quite a comfortable vehicle is the droshky but for the fact that the drivers always seize any opportunity to whip or worry their horses. On arrival at the offices we went to a room where an official examined our papers. In less than a minute he endorsed the club certificate, and with a smile, said, " Good luck ! "

Next we went to the harbour police, where our passports were stamped. The officer went to see his chief and came back with the news that we could leave when we wished. There was not even to be a Customs examination for a British yacht !

The young man who had assisted us was in a transport of delight. A continual smile played about his mouth, and in his enthusiasm he could not keep still for a moment.

"Like an American, I am," he said : "time is money. Time is money !" I agreed, inwardly thinking how much money he must lose, for he seemed to do little but hang about the hotel.

We went back to the ship before lunch, after which Sehmel and I were very busy finishing off the rigging and making final preparations for sea. In the afternoon we tried to start the engine but, as I had suspected, it showed no signs of life, and we waited for the arrival of an engineer who, in a moment of wisdom, had been engaged in advance ; but as he did not appear our plan to sail next morning had to be abandoned.

It was a Tuesday, the 30th of July, that dawned in a very ordinary way as many Tuesdays in July have dawned before and will dawn again. The barometer was 30·1, the wind west. As a matter of fact we did not see the dawn for, enthusiastic as we were, we found six o'clock early enough to turn out. The engineer arrived at seven and he remained till five in the evening, by which time the ship smelt of oil, the companion was black with dirt, and the engineer, who in the morning had been a fair-haired young man, looked more like a nigger. At times the engine emitted strange noises, then calmed down and silence reigned. Everything was peaceful except in my mind, for the wind was steady and moderate ; and a day was lost. At 5 p.m. I knelt in the mess and learned to guide the ill-willed brute which was now emitting fiendish but continuous noise. At 6.30 Sehmel arrived, the sails were set, and the ship deliberately sailed away. A cheer was raised by Sehmel's wife and by

Sehmel's children, but silence reigned supreme over the yacht club round the corner.

Our voyage had commenced, and at last we were away gliding through the clean water past the reeds. Care was lifted from our shoulders, for we were free from advice, pessimism, officialism, heat and hot air. Sehmel was at the helm piloting the ship he was so soon to lose. Rather a pathetic old man he looked. *Annette* moved slowly in the light evening air, and the sun, now low in the sky, touched the waves with gold that accentuated the darkness of the trees on the shore. By the time it had fallen behind a lurking cloud *Annette* had left the lake and passed through a narrow reed-bound channel into the deep fairway of the Muhlgraben. To port ran a straight line of wharves, backed by empty warehouses and workmen's cottages, and to starboard a mass of floating timber was penned in by wood staging. We ate in rather a subdued way, and the old man unfolded some of his past history in the peculiar quiet even voice that is his. The sky to the west was tinged with pink, and soon against that peaceful background there rose the gaunt spectacle of a great roofless building. This, once the largest shipbuilding yard in Riga, had been burnt down in the war, and now nothing but the walls remain ; the roof, the windows, chimneys, and frames have been gutted by fire. It was as impressive a scene as could be imagined—a grim scar bearing memories of the past and perhaps a warning for the future. The old man told us more about his town. It had suffered greatly in recent years ; had been sacked by German and Russian in turn, and was now but a ghost of its former prosperity. Even the homes of the workmen employed in the great yard were being pulled to bits for the sake of the bricks, and the

Muhlgraben, once busy, was, when we passed, deserted save for one solitary steamer.

It was dark when we got into the Dvina River, but the moon was up to silver the water and guide us down the river. The current also helped us, so not very much time elapsed before we took a turn to port and tied up in the winter harbour at the entrance of the river.

Early next morning footsteps and scratchings overhead disturbed my dreams, and I realised the old man was walking about instead of sleeping. A little thought enabled me to understand the mystery, for it had only been at the last moment that Sehmel had decided to sleep on board, and so his bed—although composed of ropes and sails by no means akin to thorns—was far from perfect. This explained his early rising, and in sympathy I ought to have got up to join him in his exercise. I did nothing of the sort, however, but slept on until six.

After a quick breakfast we bade farewell to Sehmel, rowing him ashore in the little dinghy. We were then truly on our own : in a foreign port with a strange ship, with charts, provisions, and money with which to find our way home by our own unaided efforts. The old man stood watching as I hoisted the dinghy to the foredeck, turned it over and lashed it down. Then the mizzen was hoisted, the staysail made ready. Two minutes of hard work and up came the anchor black with mud, the headsail filled, and the " crew " steered *Annette* towards the harbour entrance into the Dvina. The Customs outlook was passed, but no restraining shout was raised, for the harbour police had telephoned through warning them to expect a little English yacht that was free to leave. Sehmel stood there waving his arm until he was almost out of sight, and the ship, with all sail set, was carried by the strong current out past the pier heads.

The wind was south-west and moderate in force ; and a course was set to pick up the western coast of the Gulf of Riga, about half-way from its northern extremity, near a point named Messargotsem. That was at 9.15 in the morning, but the ship sailed slowly and, as the rain held off for but a short time, it was fated that the day's run should be nothing on which we might congratulate ourselves. The wind was uncertain both in force and direction ; one moment it would be a gentle breeze with the ship scarcely moving, but the next a dark-blue cloud, like a great mushroom from sea to sky, might be seen approaching. The breeze would strengthen into a wind, then to a squall, until it was dispersed by heavy rain, and once more the ship would be scarcely moving. At 7.30 a calm, definite and enraging, settled down and the sun made its appearance for the first time.

The engine ? Yes, what an excellent chance for testing its efficiency. I removed the companion steps that veiled its oily glory and started a blow lamp that for a considerable time refused to blow ; but at length a steady roar broke the silence of an otherwise perfect evening. Fumes arose from the companion. All was efficient and mechanical— smell and noise. In ten minutes I turned on the paraffin, the water and the lubricating oil, and gave the flywheel a couple of half-turns. A furious din ensued, and there was no question that the motor was going. Skipper and crew ascended and solemnly watched the sea. Was the ship moving ? We thought she was, but we were not sure. Presently a piece of seaweed hove in view and was left behind in what business men call " due course." Then the motor stopped as suddenly as it had started ; and we gratefully packed it away.

Now, as we then were making West, by calculation Messargotsem Point should have been about abeam, some miles to port. As a matter of fact it was abeam but some miles to starboard. The explanation was easy, for the compass was situated near the "smelly monster," and naturally refused to behave properly. From *Annette's* last owner I had heard a whisper about deviation, but amongst the gear I had been unable to find a deviation card ; and Sehmel had thought the matter in some way had been put right. To confirm this I had tested it as she lay in the harbour pointing North, and had found it approximately right. Now that our course had been north-west I found it most certainly and most damnably wrong, so it was not until one-thirty next morning that we anchored for the night two miles south-west of the missing point.

At five-thirty sleep was disturbed. Sounds of rowing were unmistakable. The sounds ceased and I listened, knowing that a boat was close to us, if not actually alongside. Out of a porthole I espied a long narrow fishing boat, manned by three most ruffianly looking men. It was time to put in an appearance so, carefully brushing my hair to dispel any suggestion of sleep, I went on deck assuming the expression of a hunter for early worms. They offered to sell fish, but on refusal rowed away, so that I was able to sleep on for an hour.

We breakfasted and made sail at nine, soon passing the village from which the fishermen came. It was not unlike a native settlement in appearance as the huts were roughly constructed of wood, and surrounded by a sort of light-coloured palisade that showed up strongly in contrast with the dark forest. The wind was westerly and the weather similar to that of the previous day : squalls, calms and thunder.

During the afternoon many of the mushroom storms passed, darkening the sky, and in the evening a waterspout passed in the north causing us some unnecessary anxiety. We sailed slowly, but the coast was not uninteresting ; sandy, fringed by a few low trees and backed by an unending belt of forest. It was not until 1.30 a.m. next day that we dropped anchor to the south of Dome Ness, the north-western extremity of the Gulf of Riga. Thus with endless energy we had sailed sixty miles in two long days. The last of the wind before it fell off had been east, so there was a chance of doing better in the near future.

On this cruise it was fated that we should sail by night as much as by day—from misfortune not wilfulness. *Annette* carried but 420 square feet of canvas, and needed a fresh breeze to log even three knots. As her motor was then unsatisfactory, this meant that we had to sail continually to make any progress worthy of mention ; and also that in order to take advantage of the heavy wind that suited her it was necessary to sail in bad seas that kept ships of many times her size in port.

The fishing village near Dome Ness was small, just a few wooden huts and an occasional farm. It was Sunday, and all the boats were hauled out along the shore, while their owners slept or talked in groups as is the manner of seafaring folk. A coastguard had espied a strange sight shadowing the regular peace of his domain. It was a ship small and white, of unusual proportions: no fishing, no trading boat that ; yet there she lay at anchor waiting for something ! Through the coastguard's brain the thought probably passed that she was waiting a fair wind to carry out some obscure but possibly improper business. If he had been an energetic man he would have rowed out to make cautious enquiries, but instead of this he remained where he was, throwing stones into the sea until as luck would have it his chance came ; for a little varnished dinghy put out from the stranger and approached his sacred land.

We ran the boat ashore at the point where the coast-guard was waiting to meet us, and showed our passports as we read officialdom in his khaki coat and grey trousers. He could not speak English, but apparently he judged we were harmless, for he handed the papers back with a smile; and, in answer to an enquiry, led us over the sand dunes to a little farm where we were able to buy milk and eggs. He then left us to our own devices.

The day was fine and sunny, but a fresh wind swept up from the west, preventing sailing. The coast had looked fascinating, so *Annette* had been anchored close in, and we had come ashore with the object more of exploring than provisioning. The second nature, that makes islands attractive and induces otherwise sane persons to throw stones into the sea, called us towards the Point; so we set out along the shore in a northward direction. We passed a landing-stage which had collapsed in places, and a few minutes' walk along the hard shore brought us near the Head, where, for a moment, we left the sea to strike inland. Remains of railway lines, and deep trenches now overgrown with weed, betrayed signs of fortification; and presently we came on a tower, or rather the shell of a tower, for the top of it had been blown off and the base was pitted with shell holes. A stone's throw away stood the bare walls of a house, roofless and blackened. Near this were ruins of other buildings. Thus the results of an advanced " civilisation " had visited even that remote part of the world, where on the bright summer's day, with the sea in sight and the blue waves whispering, it would have been difficult to imagine the vibration of artillery and the glare of fire— difficult but for the sudden sight of desolate remains of what once had been the homes of men.

We returned to where we had left the dinghy, and, sheltered from the wind by a sand bank, we passed time in writing and sketching. At 7.30 we had dinner on the ship, and after washing up played the gramophone—a new toy bought at Riga. While thus engaged we failed to notice the arrival of two boats which hovered round listening to the music, and it was not until the sound of one of them rowing away caught our attention that we noticed the other. She was a typical Lettish fishing boat, narrow, with high bow and stern, having an appearance most piratical. Her crew of three youths looked harmless enough, so I asked them to come alongside, offering cigarettes and a drink. My wife produced the bottle of vodka purchased at Riga, so, as I was anxious to find out how it was drunk, I placed it on deck together with a jug of water, signing them to help themselves. The eldest took the bottle and emptied most of the contents into a large mug, then added water and, with the assistance of a friend, finished the lot. Next he drained the remainder of the bottle. Thus in my method of learning the fashion in drinking it I lost all the vodka I possessed.

The youngest did not join in this celebration, and, as he neither drank nor smoked, my wife offered him a chocolate. It was a most insulting thing to do, involving him in so much ridicule from his companions that if any vodka had been left his good resolutions would most certainly have been broken.

The hearts of the youths were warmed up considerably by this liberal dose of alcohol, and we carried on a lot of conversation about ships and fishes. I showed them what fishing tackle we possessed, and asked by signs how it should be used. It was a little tin sardine with a number of hooks hidden in red rag. They lowered it about a yard into the water and the one holding the line jerked his hand rapidly whilst his companions, wildly excited, peered down into the sea until their boat looked on the point of turning over. I had fished at odd moments from yachts for several years, but, owing to unsuitable bait, the sum total of my catch had only amounted to two mackerel, a crab, and my wife's finger ; so my surprise can be imagined when before even a minute had elapsed the youth gave a shout and a pull at his line. The others in a state of great excitement leant over until the water almost poured aboard. What a catch ! A long powerful silvery form threshed the water, then disappeared. We waited to see it pulled aboard, but, sad to relate, the line came home true enough, but fish, lead, bait ?—none !

There was no bait left on board, but our friends, whose activity was fired by sport and possibly by spirit, set off towards the shore at a most remarkable speed to get some of what they called " sprottes." They were soon back and gave us a number of little fish—sprats. We fancied we were to be up all night fishing, but they made us understand that their present was for eating, not for bait, and they soon departed and we turned in.

CROSSING THE BALTIC, GOTLAND AND OLAND

CHAPTER IV

TO get up early in the morning is a feat requiring no little will power, unless artificial aid is available, but on August 3rd this necessary impetus arrived at 4 a.m. in the shape of a boat alongside. It was the fisher boys who had come to present us with a bucket of sprats; but, as there was little wind, we turned in again after they had gone and did not make sail before nine.

From Dome Ness a sand-bank runs out in a north-easterly direction for some miles, and at the end of this spit stands a lighthouse. As the breeze was so light it took no less than three hours to bring this abeam. A schooner of rakish appearance was lying at anchor there provisioning the occupants of the lonely islet. We slipped slowly past her, and then altered course to follow the coast; and a nice little breeze sprang up from the east.

Skipper and crew were not on the usual friendly terms, as a third party in the shape of a lively sprat threatened the peace. Having been presented with these miserable fish it was clearly a matter of duty to dispose of them. The cook cooked them, the skipper criticised them, the

49

crew ate them, but—the ship, the deck, the frying pan smelt of them. On top of this there was labour trouble, resulting in a conspiracy to make the skipper wash up. The remainder of the sprats left over from breakfast were eventually thrown overboard, as it was decided that they were not worth the rent of the saucepan. In spite of this opinion, however, we towed two lines for mackerel; as we hoped to have the pleasure of fishing without the annoyance of catching anything. Our hopes were gratified.

The day passed slowly as the ship sailed steadily but slowly along the coast. At frequent intervals it was thought that the last point before the open Baltic was in sight, but on each occasion further trees appeared in the distance, floating as it were in mist. That is the peculiarity of a low coast when the visibility is poor. Objects a long way off come into sight in a quite haphazard manner, the more distant part often becoming discernible before the nearer coast, giving the impression of islands fog-bound. The coast line along which we were passing was rather beautiful. The sea was edged with sand dunes backed with scrub which protected the great dark woods that formed the background. It was a wild vicinity with scarcely a sign of habitation : a veritable refuge for the wolves and woodcutters that gripped the imagination in days of childhood.

During the day the wind slowly backed until it steadied a little west of north, and the glass fell a tenth. Not wishing to lose time we did not make for shelter, but carried on, and by ten at night we were clear of the eastern coast of the Baltic and heading right across for the Swedish island of Gotland, some hundred miles to the west. All night the wind freshened and our ship lashed fiercely forward in the dark, and when the glow of dawn lightened the sky half a gale was blowing. That was of course our first experience of *Annette* in the open sea, and we found she behaved magnificently, treating the heavy waves with scorn. We hove-to for breakfast and then sailed on all day. It was exhilarating work with a rattling breeze in the sails, and spray flying at each plunge of the ship as she strained forward on her course. Land lay far below the horizon, and we were happy, for the day was very beautiful. Clouds raced across the sky, and sometimes black squalls, purpling the sea and bringing deluges of rain, would appear in the distance, and swiftly pass over. Then the sun would break through and a rift of blue would appear between the dark masses above ; and the colour of the sea would deepen, save where the breaking waves flecked it with long white seething scars. It was deep water there, the deepest in the Baltic, and in parts the lead could have dropped ninety fathoms full, had we a line long enough, and the time to take the sounding.

Time slipped by and the ship steadily thrust forward, leaving mile after mile of open water astern. It was a grand passage, a real deep ocean voyage for our ship ; and when, towards the fall of evening, distant land piled itself up against the clouds on the horizon, we experienced a feeling of utter happiness. Our exact position, however, we could not determine owing to the inaccuracy of the compass, and, since the coast of Gotland is surrounded by reefs and shoals, the question involved was one of more than casual interest. From the lie of the land compared with the chart we thought we were a little to the south of Ostergarns ; but, as it turned out, we need not have worried, for the wind fell and it was dark before we were close to the shore, when the flash of a lighthouse confirmed our calculation.

The glass had fallen another tenth ; the sunset had been more beautiful than comforting; and, when darkness fell, the moon glimmered pallid and damp through the enshrouding clouds. It was a certain warning and, as might have been expected, a gale was blowing before midnight. We hove-to under the lee of the land with short canvas, and

THE COAST OF GOTLAND SURROUNDED BY REEFS
AND SHOALS

turned in. The duty of going on deck every hour to see everything was in order fell on the skipper; but as we had been sailing all through the previous night this duty was arduous and far from easy to remember; and at some time in the hours of early morning I fell asleep. The ship meanwhile sailed her sweet way, leaving the deep sea and picking her way over a reef until a lighthouse stood quite close. It was at this moment that the cook in a fit of energy got up to get breakfast. She far exceeded her duties and woke up the skipper; with the result that *Annette* turned her stern to the land in a remarkably quick time and headed out to sea. A gale of wind was still blowing and we sailed north intending to make Katthammarsvik harbour ; but, as it was a head wind, we put into a little bay and made towards a place marked on the chart as Ljugarn. By the time we had come abeam of the pier a pilot put off and showed us a hundred yards to the harbour, for which assistance he charged ten shillings.

When cruising abroad quays are to be avoided, as a crowd rapidly gathers and instead of decreasing after normal curiosity should have been long satisfied, it increases until by sunset it is difficult from the ship to see anything but a mass of faces, mute and staring. The friendlier the people the larger the crowd. Ljugarn was no exception to the rule, but as the village was small and scattered the onlookers were not so numerous as elsewhere, and came at different times.

We had a meal, washed, and changed our clothes before setting out on a provisioning expedition under the guidance of a civil engineer who was on holiday from Stockholm. He spoke English perfectly and made it his duty to do everything he could to help us. The village was not particularly pretty, as it consisted merely of a few fishing huts and pensions, but the visitors there, mostly from Stockholm, were an exceptionally nice lot. In the afternoon we were quite disappointed with our first impression of Sweden, where nothing appeared very different from England, but at 7 o'clock we went to an hotel where our civil engineer friend had arranged for our dinner. A little old lady bowed us into a private room and then disappeared into the kitchen, where her shrill voice could be heard raised on high in heated admonition of the servants. Presently a vast assortment of food was brought in on separate dishes: a sort of glorified *hors d'œuvre* fortified by fried eggs. This seemed enough for an evening meal but, when our appetites were almost satisfied, the maid entered and, with a shy but charmingly old-fashioned curtsey, placed a large course of chicken and vegetables before us. The little old lady hovered behind, smiling in admiration at the quantity of food the English could put away. The chicken was no sooner finished and cleared away, than the maid entered and, after her usual curtsey, placed a final glory of raspberries and cream on the table.

It was about half-way through this repast that a young man entered ; walked straight up to me ; clicked his heels ; bowed, and said, " Herr R——." I was already getting used to foreign customs, and rose to the occasion with an almost perfect bow, but the effect was spoilt by the heels of my tennis shoes which could not be induced to click in a very convincing manner. After this introduction we divided our attention between raspberries, cream, and our new friend, who was a medical student from Stockholm. Although I cannot guarantee his knowledge of doctoring, he was certainly a mine of information on other matters. He explained that the old lady had never had English people in her hotel before, and was intent on doing justice to her country. We were dining in the room usually reserved for the visits of the Governor. He went on to tell us about the village, the people and Sweden. The news of the arrival of an English yacht had apparently spread rapidly, for we found he had already heard plenty of news of *Annette* and her crew—some of which was new even to us. It appeared, also, that we had offended some of the fishermen by locking up the ship when we left ; and we were informed that such precautions were unnecessary as everybody in Sweden was honest.

Coffee arrived—splendid coffee as the Swedes and Danes excel in making—and with the coffee came cakes. Remember that bread, hard bread, butter, milk, fish, eggs, chicken, potatoes, vegetables, cheese, sardines, cream, raspberries, beer and biscuits had already disappeared— so the reader can understand that through sheer physical lack of space we were obliged to allow the cake to live on in the light of day. The civil engineer had joined us and after dinner we went together to the pier.

It was a perfect night with a brilliant moon playing on the water and lighting the quay, which widened at its seaward end into a circular jetty, where a couple of fiddles were playing tunes to a whirling, swinging ring of dancers. Herr R—— soon disappeared, for in Sweden there are two women to every man and, as he explained, it was hardly fair not to join in. The dance was a country jig ; a jolly rollicking rhythm which made the pier echo under the stamping feet. Presently he returned, and we boarded the *Annette* to try a liqueur brought from Riga. We were taught the Scandinavian custom of drinking health, which consists of saying, " Skaäl ! " (pronounced " skole "), raising your glass, looking straight at the person whose health you are drinking and then ceremoniously replacing the glass. Feeling fairly honest although sleepy I managed to look our friends in the face, but some weeks later in Denmark it fell that I could not carry out this feat. We were drinking with a little grocer of immense pomposity ;

and we were drinking out of bottles. Just as the time came to meet the eyes of our host the fat little fellow made a noise like a chicken as he drank, and I collapsed, showing unmistakable signs of mirth.

Singing seems to be quite a national custom in Scandinavia, for we found the friends we made, whether in Sweden or Denmark, would break into song with the least provocation. Herr R—— was no exception, and, without any sign of embarrassment, gave us a number of sea chanties in Swedish and English. Curiously enough the old songs that are so rarely heard in our country are more popular than any others in Scandinavia.

The party finished at nine as the student wanted to dance, the civil engineer to go back to his hotel, and ourselves to sleep.

Next morning we repaired to the hotel for a breakfast that rivalled dinner in size, and consisted of five courses : a jug of milk over a foot high, and porridge ; herrings stewed in milk; eggs and bacon; bread; cheese and beer; coffee and cakes.

In the afternoon, as the wind had moderated, we sailed, but before leaving the question arose of how to dispose of a cheese brought from Riga which was rather conspicuous on account of its odour. It was quite good, and it seemed a pity to throw it away when times were so bad. We left it on the quay but, as we afterwards remembered the Swedish characteristic of honesty, we had grave misgivings. Probably nobody would touch what was not theirs, and in course of time it was not unlikely that the entire harbour would be in range of a very powerful smell.

The wind was light, so the ship sailed on all night to the south, before coming to anchor next morning in a little bay called Slesviken. We brought up in two different parts of the bay before finding a suitable anchorage close inshore ; and we got what sleep we could between getting sails up and down, cooking and washing up. In the afternoon a fisherman rowed off to see us, but as he did not speak English we could not follow his conversation beyond the fact that he considered *Annette* unduly beamy. His appearance solved a small domestic trouble for us in a singularly happy way. We had brought two smoked sausages from Riga. They were each about a foot long, and at first we had hung them up to the mizzen mast, but in the rough crossing the strings had broken ; and they had been put in a locker where their presence was noticeable in spite of closed doors. That morning we had sampled one with the result that most of it was thrown overboard. My wife wanted to throw the other away likewise, but I refused to agree to this as it seemed such a waste ; but the arrival of the fisherman solved the problem.

I beckoned to him and he approached with an enquiring look on his weather-beaten countenance. I then very gently lowered the sausage into his reluctant hands. This let loose a storm of language which I could not follow, and he started to row round the ship in circles at a speed not inconsiderable. He seemed suspicious about something ; and his two sons in the stern of the boat seemed amused. He presently rowed off.

The next note in the log reads, " Killed 35 flies." To be truthful, it must be admitted that my wife did this wicked deed, for I always refrain from killing flies, not from principles of kindness, but because I think they are less objectionable in their entirety than in their individual and distributed parts.

In the evening we went ashore where we were greeted by the fisherman, who patted his stomach and brought out a greasy purse. He wanted to pay for the sausage, and although I refused this he did not seem to be particularly grateful. Regarding his meal, he appeared divided between suspicion and satisfaction. I could imagine his saying, " Mad ! mad ! " We left him and skirted his house before striking inland.

The fields in Southern Gotland are divided by stone walls composed of the boulders that lie loose over the country. The land is rather unusual, being very flat and the soil peaty. Vegetation is sparse; and the most striking feature is the number of loose grey rocks, that vary in size from mere stones to huge boulders. These exist in just the same way below the surface of the sea, which shallows gradually so that the round shiny tops of rocks can be seen some distance from the shore. There is no proper demarkation of sand or cliff dividing sea from land, for the vegetation—such as it is—runs straight down to the water's edge. The shore is more like the shore on a flooded field. We walked on, climbing many stone walls, and bringing the tottering corner of one down to the ground with a crash. It did not take long to build it up, however, and we had no fear of meeting an irate landowner, for when trespassing abroad it is merely necessary to take the landowner's photograph and say, " Engleesh ! " Foreigners always like their photos to be taken, and will pose without any embarrassment.

Our walk took us into a very pretty park that might have either belonged to a large estate or have been public, and then to the village which also, in its modest way, was pretty.

We returned to the ship rather tired, but in sleep we were disappointed as a swell set into the bay; and *Annette* rolled with the particularly fiendish glee of which she is capable. Owing to this we were under way again at 4 a.m. next morning with a slight northerly wind. We did not make much progress, and at 1 p.m. the ship was still not far south of Gotland. The sea was covered with a white weed of infinite smallness, but so thick as to give the water an appearance as though diluted with milk. A constant line of great sailing ships passed all day; schooners, barques and clippers. By nightfall we found ourselves almost becalmed; so we lit our lights and hove-to. We wanted to rest, and the choice remained for us to lie-to on the starboard tack or the port tack. The former would carry us south into the line of shipping which, by the rule of the road, would have to keep clear of us; whilst the latter course would take us north clear of the shipping, but in the wrong if we got in the way of a sailing vessel on the starboard tack. We decided to adopt the latter course and at 10 p.m. turned in. Sleep under these conditions is not very restful, as every hour it is necessary to go on deck to look round for possible danger.

The wind next morning shifted to the south-east where for most of the day it remained steady but light. At 4 p.m. we saw in the distance a low ridge of the island of Oland, and went below for tea, leaving the ship to sail herself. At about five we made a literal landfall in a manner rather original; lifted the centre plate, and then fell off on the other tack. What happened exactly I will not report for fear of being called a liar.

We could not verify our position as the compass was entirely inaccurate; the deviation was about twenty degrees as far as could be guessed. We tacked slowly towards the south of the island and, when dusk fell, the triple flash of Hamnoren lighthouse gave us the clue to our position, proving us to be some miles north of our calculation. The wind had veered to south, but early the next morning it backed to south-east, enabling us to lie to Oland Rev lightship, which was passed at 8 a.m. It was blowing hard as we set the storm-jib, putting the staysail below. The glass was falling and by 11 o'clock it was blowing really hard, and there was a nasty sea running. The wind also showed a tendency to veer to the west and, as our course from Oland Rev to Upklippan lay west by south, we decided to run for a little harbour on the inner coast of Oland. It was a sound idea as the port would be under the lee of the island, but when we had run for a few miles the wind veered to south by west and strengthened to gale force. The sky was high and ribbed with white cloud, in appearance not unlike the short regular waves of a third-rate sea painting. It looked very threatening, and the wind whistled ominously. The sea was tremendous. Great combers came hissing down on the stern which leapt up to meet them. Time after time I thought they must break over, but the ship played her part and, although the breaking tops of two splashed over, no heavy water came aboard. By then it was clear that we could not run into any of the little harbours, as the shift of wind would have sent a furious breaking sea on the shallow entrances. We hove-to at once under mizzen and jib whilst there was room under our lee, for we were already embayed with the iron-bound Swedish coast to the west and the great expanse of Oland Rev to the east. It was a dangerous position, as the sea was so large as to make sailing impossible. We turned in to

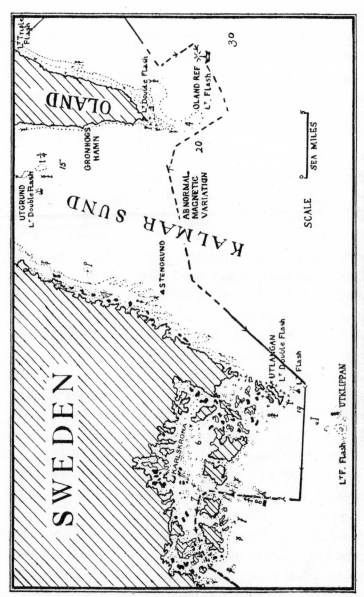

A ROUGH CROSSING FROM OLAND TO KARLSKRONA

rest and await events. There was nothing we could do and we were too tired to appreciate the grandeur of the scene—a curling, hissing mass of grey and white sea. At five the events arrived in the shape of some of the largest breakers I had up to then seen. In the pits between the waves we rolled utterly becalmed and on the summits there seemed little more than a light breeze, although the waves were white-crested. The booms banged wildly about, shaking the yacht from stem to stern. The motion was abominable. I hurriedly sheeted the booms in closer and took a sounding as we looked rather close to the Swedish shore. I found plenty of water; and the cause of the commotion was merely the cessation of the gale, when the sea was suddenly free of the restraining stroke of the wind. The rollers came from a hundred miles or more across the Baltic, until they were embayed in the somewhat shallow channel of sea between the island and the mainland. There they broke and twisted in all directions. There *Annette* lay rolling and pitching. There we lay trying not to be sick.

At 7 p.m. the worst was over; a light wind came from the east, steadying the ship and enabling us to lay a course for Utklippan. Extreme optimism followed deep pessimism ; and *Annette* presently bounded over the rollers, lying south to a freshening breeze. We ate a little food and the " crew " turned in for a sleep. At about midnight we passed between the island of Utlangan and the reef on which Utklippan light flashed its warning guide. It was then that a thunderstorm, that had been playing round the horizon, approached to add to the impressiveness of the black night. Thunder vibrated amongst the clouds and muttered, whilst vivid lightning from time to time lit the ship with a vicious glare. The wind veered to the south. It was my wife's watch and I turned into the cabin which was bright and cheery. It rained hard, but the crew at the helm refused to mind.

We altered course and sailed west, but as the compass was inaccurate, and there was an unlit lee shore but a few miles away, we allowed ample margin for mistakes. The margin

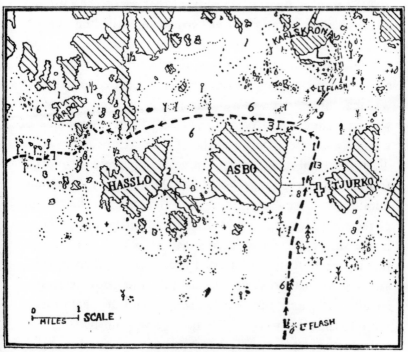

KARLSKRONA HARBOUR

was unfortunately so ample that, when at 2.30 a.m. we found by calculation that we were off Karlskrona, there were no leading lights to be seen and we hove-to, to wait for dawn before approaching the rock-lined coast. Our feelings cannot be described as anything but wretched, when we found ourselves forced to keep to sea at this early hour; but just as we were about to turn in the crew announced she thought she could see a light. As the first hint of dawn enabled us to see sufficiently to warn us of danger ahead, we at once got under way and ran towards the point where a light was suspected. The sky was gradually lightening and, just before it was too late, the crew definitely announced that she could make out ahead a regular flash.

At 4 a.m. we passed the buoys that mark the entrance to the channel leading to Karlskrona, and sailed on towards land. Two indentations appeared ahead and it was impossible to decide which was Karlskrona; so we set a compass course—not forgetting that even that instrument was inaccurate. It was blowing half a gale and a large sea was still running. Away to starboard huge fountains of white spray reared towards the sky on some sunken rock. To port several spurts of white revealed the presence of other shoals. It was anxious work, but the anxiety was of short duration as, after a few minutes had elapsed from the passing of the buoy, we espied a leading mark and saw Karlskrona in the distance. Shoal after shoal we passed, each clearly marked by beacons and a cruel breaking sea, then the ship sailed past two breakwaters and into the calm behind an island. At 7 a.m. the anchor dropped and the chain roared out into the clear water. The passage was finished.

THE FISHERMAN'S HUT, SLESVIKEN, GOTLAND

CHAPTER V

TAKEN FOR SMUGGLERS—RED TAPE—FALSE TEETH AT A
DISCOUNT—PUSSYFOOT IN SWEDEN—COMPASS SWINGING
—THE "SMELLY MONSTER"—ON THE ROCKS—ANCHOR-
AGE AMONGST THE SKERRIES

AFTER seventy-two hours at sea, with little
sleep and indifferent food, one feels tired.
After being out in a gale one also feels tired;
so the condition of *Annette's* crew was far from
fresh. A liberal breakfast of porridge made matters better,
but it was sleep that was most needed. Before we had rested
an hour, peace was disturbed by the arrival of a Customs
launch alongside, and we were boarded by two officials.
I went on deck to see them and to show the ship's papers.
Unfortunately I had not shaved for three days, and was
wearing a very torn and dirty cricket shirt and a pair of
flannel trousers that would have disgraced a tramp. Other
little deficiencies, such as the absence of shoes and socks,
evidently made a bad impression on the two men.

They could not understand English and evidently could
not understand English ways; for the whole ship seemed
to be an object of the utmost suspicion. To cut short a
long story, we argued in different languages for an hour,
at the end of which it became clear that nothing would
induce them to leave *Annette* in peace. The senior of the
two was quite civil, but evidently worried; whilst the other,
whom I fancy was but an engineer, was offensive in manner

and constantly pointed to his brass buttons repeating, " Kongelig," which I was aware meant royal. I felt rather like pointing to our burgee flying in the breeze and saying, " Kongelig," but I was too painfully aware that my face and clothes would have discounted any prestige due to the regal aspect of the bunting. In short, he was an ignorant, self-important little scamp, full of the arrogance of third-rate officialdom; but I must admit that he worsted me, as he seemed prepared to argue by signs all day, and I was in no mood for talking. They decided we must at once proceed to the inner harbour to be examined, and as I refused to sail they gave us a tow-rope.

Now we had not a workable capstan, and, as the water was deep, it required considerable effort to raise the sixty-pound anchor and thirty feet of iron chain and simultaneously to break the anchor out of its bed. Without having any means of obtaining a purchase, I soon found that the direct strain was too much for me alone in the condition that I was then in—particularly when the cause of all the trouble was sitting idly watching. The launch came back and the engineer came aboard and, with a great show of superior strength, proved his extra help sufficient to do the deed. He returned to his launch and I took *Annette's* helm whilst she was towed down the narrow channel to the harbour. It was warm and sunny, and would have been pleasant under ordinary circumstances; but when tired one is apt to be depressed.

Karlskrona is of course the great naval port of Sweden. It is built on an island and its large harbour is protected by outlying islands, two of which are joined by an artificial barrier. From the south entrance to the inner harbour where *Annette* was being towed it was about a couple of miles. It must not be imagined that this enclosed area is anything like an English harbour. On the contrary it is a small sea dotted with little barren islets, and complicated by numberless shoals and rocks marked by beacons.

We judged the trouble we were having to be due to the fact that we came from Riga; which is not only the centre of a considerable smuggling trade, but is also the buffer between Bolshevik Russia and the outside world. Moreover, *Annette*, with her powerful sea-going lines and her dirty decks and paint, looked like a smuggler. She bore but little resemblance to a yacht, and still less did her owner look like a yachtsman. His wife? Well, she looked socially and intellectually his superior. Perhaps she wasn't his wife. Anyway, it must be inquired into. The passports were forged, maybe; and although the ship's papers looked pretty, they could not be understood.

As a matter of fact the ship was not registered in England, so that I had neither Lloyd's certificate nor an Admiralty Warrant. The papers consisted of a transfer deed, a club certificate and an insurance policy which, although sufficient, lacked the impressiveness of the more official documents. Curiously enough it was the insurance policy that gave the Customs most satisfaction. The first word, " Whereas " was printed in heavy black type and seemed to fascinate them. They read it out slowly—" W H E R E A S." They scratched themselves and read it again. I jumped to the occasion, nodded, smiled and repeated " WHEREAS." My wife said, " Whereas "; and we all shook hands. There was no doubt that the papers were all right.

In spite of this, however, our ship was towed off for examination, and we were most unhappy. They anchored us near some yachts, where they left us so that they might

report the matter to their seniors. I seized the opportunity
to shave and wash. We donned our best clothes and waited,
conscious that the difficulty was probably thus solved.

At various times we saw them watching us from a quay,
but the morning passed and at midday they and their launch
disappeared. Whatever trouble it might afterwards cause
us, we determined to go ashore for a good meal. Accordingly we launched the dinghy and rowed over to a landing-
stage where some other boats and yachts lay. It was
evidently a sort of naval training school, so we asked a
bearded sailor to look after the dinghy ; and then we set
off up a hill for the town.

It was not far to the shops, but no sooner had we found
these than a sailor ferreted us out, and signified that a man
with many stripes on his arm wanted us to return and
remove our dinghy from the naval steps. As other members
of the public were allowed this privilege, I was rather
surprised at the lack of courtesy to a foreign yachtsman.
We returned and found the aggrieved officer watching our
boat with an expression of injured dignity. He could not
speak English, but he left no doubt of his meaning ; so
I silenced him by pointing to the boat, then to the horizon,
and bowing deeply in a manner that did anything but
appease his injured feelings. We embarked and he walked
off, his sword rattling. We rowed round to the town steps
and left the boat where it was at the mercy of the children.

We then walked back to the town and, in a state far from
amiable, went into an hotel where we fortunately found a
waiter who could speak English. The hotel is said to be
one of the best, and is certainly the most expensive in Karlskrona. The restaurant is a long room of gloomy appearance,
with big glass windows on the left which open into a court,

where there is a band and a number of chairs and tables for coffee. Our attention was drawn both orally and visually by the way in which people were eating their food. Never had we seen such appetites. A middle-aged lady sat erect at the next table, but her noble appearance was marred by the avidity with which she devoured the food, and the enthusiasm with which she got up to select further supplies from a large table which, in accordance with the Swedish custom, was loaded with a selection of eatables. False teeth in that town must be at a discount, for food appears not to be bitten, but swallowed whole in huge lumps.

After lunch we went to a bank where manners were also typical of Karlskrona. We found the true exchange to be about 18 kroner to the pound, and wished we had been there before, as at the hotel they had only given us 16·50, the waiter being apparently not content with selling an expensive meal and getting a good tip.

This was our first and last sight of a large Swedish town, and I believe it was a poor example. The people there seemed quite different from the Stockholmer's at Ljugarn, or any other Swedes met before or since. Elsewhere we found the Swedish charming, and wanting neither in courtesy nor manners. A further peculiarity of Karlskrona is the comparative rarity of the blonde. Judging from the population one would not think it was a town of the North.

Having already come into disagreeable touch with a bank, an hotel, the Customs and Navy, we decided it was time to put in an appearance at the British Consulate before the Customs or the Admiralty authorities locked us up as smugglers or spies. If, hitherto, we had been victims of red tape and ill-mannered officials, it was compensated by the kindness of the Vice-Consul, who was, of course, a

Swede. He phoned up the Customs and learnt that we were free of all formality. Not even our passports required to be stamped, and the fuss in the morning was apparently due to the anxiety of two underlings to prove their devotion to duty. The Consul arranged for our motor to be repaired and our compass to be swung. His lady secretary spent all the next morning helping my wife to shop, and no trouble was too much for her. For example, we could not get whisky, as spirits are unprocurable in Sweden without a card. The cards are only issued to registered citizens who have attained twenty-seven years of age, and who have paid their taxes; and then the quantity allowed to each person is limited to four litres a month—quite a fair amount one would think! We ourselves could only have procured spirits after a great deal of formality had not the Consul very kindly helped by buying a bottle of whisky for us off his own card. It was most necessary to have some spirits on board, as teetotalism, when cruising under cold, wet and difficult conditions, is simply an invitation to pneumonia.

We were three days at Karlskrona, in which time we thoroughly provisioned the ship, and induced an engineer to repair the "smelly monster." The trouble seemed to be that the paraffin never reached the cylinder, and the matter was easily put right, so that on our last day, before leaving the town, we were proudly able to proceed under auxiliary power, with two opticians in order to have the compass swung. We anchored in the roads near a fine full-rigged ship in which Swedish youth is trained for the navy. She looked very trim and smart and her crew very seamanlike.

Compass swinging is an operation with which most people interested in the sea are familiar. The process with large ships and small ships is the same, except that in the case of the latter there is manual labour to be done. *Annette's* stern had to be towed round by the dinghy so that her bows swung slowly to every point of the compass. This work, which involved a certain amount of physical exertion, fell on me, much to my disgust; for the attention of one of the opticians was taken in making observations and shouting, whilst the other checked the compass and made notes. It was a long process, and the morning had passed before I was free to come aboard. The observations had proved the deviation to be up to 24°, with a maximum at about west and a minimum a little east of north. It was a relief to know the error exactly, for up to then we had not found it possible to lay an accurate course—a miserable state of affairs.

The anchor was raised and I tackled the angelic motor. It started without hesitation and the ship moved—backwards. I altered the reverse, and it stopped. Two hard swings of the flywheel and it was going again—still backwards. The opticians peered down at me with respectful misgivings. Once again I altered the lever and *Annette* moved—backwards. By this time considerable excitement was noticeable on the faces watching my efforts. A light breeze had carried the ship out of the channel and a rocky islet appeared a few yards to leeward. The solution was simple really, for all that was necessary was to let the ship have her way and proceed backwards. This we did and returned towards the harbour, stern first. It was an original method; and passing ships apparently found it amusing, so I was thankful when, after a lot of trouble, I was successful in inducing it to work in a manner more conventional. We were soon at anchor in our old position; and I rowed the opticians ashore. Their charge was quite moderate, and they were extremely civil and obliging. My wife thought they were naval, as they wore a uniform with " Kongelig " on the buttons. Whether her opinion was correct will never be known; but in appearance and manner they were like petty officers of British training.

The next day, August 15th, we started at 10 a.m. The wind was south-west and the weather warm and settled. We left the harbour under the motor which, in the absence of an engineer, moved with the energy of a British workman. I did not mind so long as *Annette* moved at all ; but as the crew did not approve—feeling it lacked dignity to be on a ship that made so much fuss and so little progress—I cheered the "smelly monster" to further efforts, and *Annette* moved a trifle faster than before, whilst fish came to the surface—stunned with the 800 shocks per minute.

To be serious, however, the engine really did make a very great din; so much so that it effectually prevented any communication between the crew, who was steering, and myself, who was supposed to be navigating.

With a heavy bump the ship crashed. I dashed on deck and saw a number of yellow rocks under us and a beacon to starboard. I shouted to my wife to steer for this, and hurried forward to lower sails; but no sooner had I dropped the mainsail than the bumping ceased and we were in deep water. It was the motor, the blessed "smelly monster," that had pulled us off. We anchored to think, for, according to our chart, which was of diminutive scale, we had been right in leaving the beacon to starboard.

We could not find our error, and to this day the problem is unsolved.

After this little incident we caged the motor in a wooden box and started to sail seriously. There was a pleasant light wind, and everything was very enjoyable in the bright summer day. Navigation was most interesting, for we had to thread our way between the islands and the rocky patches. These latter were marked by beacons, but the question always arose as to which side they were to be left. The Swedish system of buoyage is complicated and misleading to strangers, and our chart was on a very small scale. We soon passed the island behind which we had anchored on the morning of our arrival at Karlskrona. Our course then lay to the west and we had to tack. It was five miles to the entrance of the harbour, and this we passed in the late afternoon. We then dropped the mainsail, so as to move slowly whilst I took frequent soundings, and my wife navigated the ship past a large rock, unmarked on the chart, to an excellent little anchorage under the lee of an island.

The chain roared out, and *Annette* lay comfortably moored for the night in a small bight, almost landlocked. A stone's throw away was the island, uninhabited, almost barren; to the north stretched the shore of what we called the mainland, but which we afterwards learnt was but another island; to the east lay yet another skerry, on which a cow fed in solitary state; and from the south we were protected at a distance of about half a mile by one of the outer isles, and at a distance of twenty yards by a shiny rock, on the top of which sparse vegetation eked out a precarious existence.

Whilst the sails were being made up, a small trading ship, flying a German flag, passed close and dropped anchor in evident haste. A boat was launched and rowed off to the mainland, where its crew, having made it fast, strode up a green terrace to what looked like a farm-house. Presently they returned carrying something, which we guessed was a cargo of farm produce, rowed back to their ship, and immediately got under way again.

We had a small meal before setting out to the nearest island to explore.

The dinghy scrunched on the stony shore and we jumped out and walked towards the centre. The island was composed of granite thinly covered by dry grass, and dotted with furze bushes, stunted growth and moss-covered boulders. The land rises in the middle to a little hill surmounted by a beacon and scarred by a trench. The view is magnificent, and in the evening light, in which we saw it, a more romantic place would be hard to imagine: the well-treed " mainland " backed by distant hills to the north, and the broken contours of numberless islets and reefs in every other direction. The little ship that was our home lay mirrored in the sea, and the yellow light of early evening tinged the whole scene, save where distance added a softness to its glare. A slight surf from the open sea whispered to windward.

The crew made a sketch and the skipper took a nap.

Towards dusk we returned to the ship for a pail in which to put milk, and then we rowed towards the " mainland." The water soon shallowed, but a little creek opened up, and led to a moss-covered landing stage of diminutive size. We tied the dinghy up to some bushes and followed a path which skirted a field, and then guided us past the green terrace to the house where we had seen the men go earlier in the afternoon. A few farm buildings came into sight and relieved us of embarrassment ; for up to then we had not felt quite sure whether our destination might not prove to be a private house. We walked up a few steps to a verandah where some women were talking, and asked for milk. They could not speak English, but it was not difficult to explain what we wanted by signs, and after a short wait the pail was filled for us. Meanwhile the farmer arrived and introduced himself; but, as he likewise spoke only Swedish, little conversation ensued. He did not impress us with feelings of either respect or liking; and possibly he realised this for, with a magnificent sweep of the hand, he indicated that he was the owner of all the surrounding land.

When he left he accompanied us with his wife, and showed us some pike and eels that he had caught. They came on board for a few minutes, and we were glad when they went, for we were tired and they were uninteresting and inquisitive.

" HOVE TO "

CHAPTER VI

A THREATENING EVENING—A FINE SAIL BY NIGHT——MUSIC OF
THE HISSING WAVE——SKILLINGE——AN OLD SALT——THE
"SMELLY MONSTER" AGAIN——CALM AT SOUTH-EAST
FALSTERBO POINT——LARGE DINNER AND GOOD——THE
VOYAGE OF THE DINGHY

NEXT morning there was not much wind; but we set sail early, and slipped out between the rock and the island, keeping a keen look-out for sunken reefs. The yacht was soon out of shelter and bobbing to the swell; but, although we were clear of the actual entrance to Karlskrona, there were yet many islets and shoals to be avoided before we could gain deep water. Our chart, let me repeat, was very small and only marked a few of the beacons, and we soon found navigation was even more difficult than anticipated. After making two short tacks between two islands we almost wished that we had taken the advice of the marine opticians, who had advised us on no account to leave by the western entrance without a pilot. It was then that we noticed a small white yacht overtaking us, and we sailed slowly so that she might pass and lead the way through the channel. The plan worked perfectly, and we were soon following them and congratulating ourselves on our luck; for the passage was very complicated, sometimes perhaps a mile wide and in places but a few yards. It would have been difficult to have picked our way through, guided alone by the patches of water breaking on sunken shoals; for in more than one point the correct channel was but a few feet from a patch of breaking water.

The wind was light and unfavourable, so that *Annette* had not much to help her over the swell that was still running from the wind of the previous day. For twenty-four hours we made tack after tack, each several miles long. It was not unpleasant, for during the whole day the sky and sea remained a deep blue colour unshadowed by passing cloud. On the inshore tacks we could make out the coast, but as it was composed of islets and outlying rocks it was not wise to approach it close. The day passed, and at dusk we had made only about twenty miles westward.

The evening was most impressive, as by then in the west there hung great banks of dark cloud that were tinged by the sun setting behind the black hump of Hanö Island. The sky to the east also was overcast; the glass had fallen; and the voice of the wind in the shrouds loudened into a warning of approaching storm. Presently a light flashed out from the top of Hanö, and we knew our last hopes of a night in harbour were shattered, for the nearest port lay behind the island and was protected by two unlit shoals; and, although the granite mass of Hanö offered protection, we found by reference to the chart that the shores were steep-to on the south-west, offering no anchorage.

The wind soon freshened to half a gale, but as our new course lay more to the south it was abeam, and the sea, being off-shore, was only moderate. The night was black without a hint of a moon, but in the rifts between the clouds stars shone out. I took watch, and the ship foamed on her way crashing through the short seas to the music of hissing wave and shrilling rigging. Thus the hours slipped by and we drove fiercely forward on our course through the darkness. The bay was crossed almost before we realised it for, in the very early hours of the following morning, long before daylight, we almost ran aground on the coast the other side. I forget now how it happened, but for some reason we had failed to pick up the lighthouse, and whilst trying to make it out we became aware of lights above us, and at the same time realised that what we had taken for the flickering light of a fishing boat was a buoy warning us of some danger. A cast of the lead proved we were in shallow water, although it was so dark that not a hint of land could be seen. The course was altered and the ketch fled south under the pilotage of the crew past Stens Head ; and, when dawn came and with it moderation in the wind, the lightening sky showed land near at hand.

It was Sunday, and as we were cold, and both the ship and ourselves drenched from flying spray, we decided we had earned rest. The wind, however, fell away; and it took an hour before we were close enough to the shore to anchor. We turned in and slept until 1 p.m.

After lunch we made sail again; but, as the new course was westerly, and the wind had shifted to that point and freshened, we had to tack for the two miles to the nearest port. The coast line consisted of hilly, green fields running almost down to the rocky shore. Farms and occasional clumps of trees relieved the monotony. The chart marked the coast as practically steep-to, but when we were close to Skillinge—a little fishing village mentioned in the Baltic Pilot—we saw rocks ahead, and the lead recorded but a fathom. The helm went down and *Annette* swung head to wind whilst I hurriedly dropped anchor. Two piers clearly marked the entrance, but as rocks seemed liberally distributed on each side we did not feel disposed to enter, until a pilot, in a white boat, rowed off and navigated us through the narrow channel into harbour. He was a very capable man, for when the time came to lower sail I found the wet halyards—which were too large for the blocks—had jammed, so that the mainsail would not come down, and the pilot

OFF THE SOUTH COAST OF SWEDEN

From Karlskrona to the little fishing village of Skillinge

had to use his brains quickly. He did not lose his head, and sailed round the harbour until finally he brought up *Annette* head to wind alongside the inmost quay.

I suppose quite thirty people had assembled to meet the yacht and assist in bringing her up; so, without any work on my part, the ropes and fenders were adjusted, and sails and halyards made up. A Customs official, who could speak English, arrived and made a short but genuine examination of the yacht. He advised us to go to Simrishamn, a little town ten miles away, to get our passports stamped, as until this was done there would be an examination at every port.

Most of the onlookers were able to speak English. We made the acquaintance of an old retired sea captain, who showed us over the village and also helped us buy provisions. He was a typical old salt who had sailed the world over, and amassed sufficient savings to buy a couple of ships of his own to provide a source of income for his old age. He was very proud of his village, not on account of any claims to beauty or antiquity, but because of its new houses and new schools. In the evening he took us to see his home. We were anxious to see the interior of a Swedish house, as we thought perhaps some little peculiarities might exist, but his little home was like that of any other sea captain, complete to its piano and pictures of ships. As elsewhere in Sweden music was the household accomplishment, and the captain's daughter played the piano and gave us a song.

We stayed two days at Skillinge as the wind was contrary and very fresh. Numbers of trading ships found themselves similarly held up, and lay off the harbour under a shelter of the point waiting for better conditions. The captain was very anxious that we should have *Annette* put on the deck of a steamer and shipped to England, as it was so late in the year. He frankly said we should never be able to get home under our own sail. That was an opinion that we frequently heard, but chiefly from the type of person who would shirk his fair share of discomfort.

We went over by bus one day to Simrishamn and got our passports stamped. The ride by bus gave us the opportunity of seeing a little of the country, which proved to be exceedingly dull.

THE "SMELLY MONSTER" AGAIN

After two days in the harbour, although the villagers were extremely good to us, we became very tired of being the one object of attention. The greater part of a day was spent in attempting to get the "smelly monster" to work again. The head of the Customs, who was on holiday and made a hobby of engines, attended to this, and although temporarily successful he charged us nothing for his services. Such is the way in the Scandinavian villages to foreign yachtsmen; any help possible will be given as a point of hospitality: money will be refused.

One morning, August 19th, the wind veered through the north to north-east, and at midday we were ready for sea, well-provisioned. It was a great surprise to us, for earlier it had rained hard and the wind had then been still of gale force.

We decided to leave under power and, without any hesitation, the "smelly monster" roared away. The harbour was small and, as luck would have it, a sailing ship was approaching unobserved behind the pier. Just as the warps had been cast off, and *Annette* with quite unusual speed had started off stern first across the mouth of the harbour, I saw her. I pushed the reverse across and the motor promptly stopped, so that, fearing we should foul the incoming ship, I started it again backwards and *Annette* proceeded across towards the opposite quay. I then once more pulled the reverse to start the yacht forwards. The engine again stopped, and the ship, carried on by her momentum, one second later stopped also; for with a considerable crash her great broad rudder struck the quay. By then the incoming ship was safely in, and, no harm having been done, I started the motor and managed to induce *Annette* to proceed to sea bow foremost, but at a very low speed. As soon as we were clear the sails were hoisted and we slowly made towards the west. Needless to say the engine stopped in a few minutes. I cleaned the injector and then, discovering that the flywheel could be turned round completely, I applied smouldering brown paper to the hole in the cylinder for the injector ; hoping that I should be able to find a leak in the cylinder.

No success came of my efforts, so I packed the motor away.

The wind gradually backed to the west heading us off, so that at sunset we were only off Sandhammar Point, with but a few miles logged. It had been a warm sunny day, and as evening fell the sky became quite free of cloud, and a thickness in the air heralded good weather. A calm fell, and *Annette* rolled in what was left of the swell from the gale. The sea was alive with ships westward bound, for, as I mentioned before, the heavy weather had held up the great trading vessels as well as *Annette*. Around us lay a fleet of schooners with every stitch of canvas set to catch any breath of wind that might help them on their course. The horizon was dotted with topsails of ships far away to east or west, or following a line further to seaward. Occasionally a " throb-throb " would draw attention to an auxiliary passing under power with her sails quivering from the breeze caused by her own speed.

Night fell on us, and *Annette* showed as a dark mass of sail and spar against the star-flecked sky. A yellow glow shone through the port-holes and from the steering well ; the side lights burnt bright in their brackets. We lashed the helm and sailed on with immeasurable slowness. Occasionally I went on deck to see that nothing threatened our safety; but no sailing ship moved fast enough to be a source of danger, and no power ship could approach without attracting our attention by the sound of her engines and the sweep of her bow wave in the still silence of the night.

Dawn came in course of time to herald another sunny day, but the calm remained; held the next day, too, and the day after that. Ship routine went on, watch by watch, meal by meal. We made some toffee, partly to kill time, and partly because of its value as a food in bad weather that might come. On the third day the calm was even more complete than before; the sea was unruffled by even a hint of a ripple. For some hours porpoises played round the ship, and in the clear water we could see the great fish flash past at lightning speed. More than once we could see one dive near, and could follow its course through the transparent sea until it approached close to the ship, when it would shoot off at right angles and, with a sweep of a powerful tail, the grey mass would melt into green and vanish into the depths.

In three days and two nights we had only made thirty-three miles. Moreover, the ship had required almost as much attention in the light wind as she would have needed in a fresh breeze; and the price we paid in energy and work was almost as much for the thirty-three miles as it would have been for two hundred miles.

The third night slowly fell on us. The barometer was steady, and the calm so perfect that even the clouds were reflected in the glassy water. One or two ships lay near, mirrored in the water, with their sails listless, waiting; motionless. Night came on, but no sunset tinged the sea with golden glory, for the sky was mottled grey, streaked with clouds that looked like wisps of smoke floating in the heights; and the land was as a black ribbon sketched with soft charcoal. The decks were dry without a vestige of dew. It was uncanny; and as night drew on, the scene was slowly obscured, until sea and sky were wrapped in impenetrable darkness, save where an occasional light of a fishing boat flashed in near presence. But for the distant thud of a motor, or the creak of oars as a boat slid past, it was intensely quiet.

At nine everything altered. A faint but perceptible air crept up from the east, the sea was ruffled into tiny wavelets, and motion replaced stillness. The barometer was rising slightly, but all night the wind remained light, so that at 4 a.m. I—who was on watch—had only logged a few miles and just passed Smynge Head. The sea was still very slight, so I closed with the land and anchored for sleep. The wind then began to freshen, so that we had to get under way within an hour, but loss of rest in exchange for progress was a fair bargain ; and the crew presently got up, made breakfast, and took a long watch.

We were bound west as far as Falsterbo Point, where the coast of Sweden swept to the north to face Denmark, leaving the comparatively narrow Sound as a dividing ribbon of sea between the two countries. Off Falsterbo lie long fingers of sand well marked by large beacons, and also by a lightship about eight miles from the land. The wind was fresh and *Annette* seethed along her course, so that the lightship was close to port by midday. At this point all ships seemed to converge. Steamers passed constantly in northerly and southerly directions and others swung past from the east, rapidly altering course to north as they rounded the lightship. We were able to cut well inside this owing to our light draft. A full-rigged ship was slowly overhauling us, and a trading schooner was approaching from the south. *Annette* was the first to round the beacon, and fled north with the two sailing ships close on either quarter. A squall hissed down on us and the mizzen was lowered, so that within an hour we had lost the leading position, and were being hard pushed by the barge to hold the second place. The afternoon had well advanced before the spires and domes of Copenhagen could be discerned on the port bow. The low island of Saltholm was almost invisible to starboard and the Drogden lightship lay close ahead. We altered course quickly to avoid the latter, for we found a strong current setting us north. The stream of shipping was getting thicker. Great tramps and colliers steamed past, and an occasional liner slipped by. A fort appeared to port and mounds of land hardened into clearness on the other hand. By 6 o'clock we were off Copenhagen. The fortifications of the city were alongside, and ahead the white sails of a host of yachts circled about. A bewildering number of buoys had to be recognised, and, much to the delight of the crew, I found that since my last cruise in these waters I had forgotten them and had piloted *Annette* through some comparatively shallow water outside the fairway. The crew was anxious to get ashore as soon as possible; so her delight turned to rage when she discovered that I had passed the nearest entrance and had navigated the ship through the main, but more distant one.

We gybed between two miniature lighthouses at the end of the piers, and reached up in the calm water of the harbour. A long line of warehouses lay to starboard, and in no time we had left these astern and had picked up a mooring close to the tall spars of the Greenland whaler belonging to the Amateur Sail Club.

COASTING SOUTHERN SWEDEN

Whilst sailing up the Sound I had taken the opportunity to shave, but much remained to be done before we could go ashore. The sails had to be left loosely in tyers to dry, all ropes had to be coiled, and the dinghy turned over and launched. These matters took but twenty minutes, but in sailing it is the odd jobs that take the time ; just as in motoring it is the incidental expenses that run away with the pounds. It must have been about eight o'clock when at last we were free to row ashore, and by then we were naturally looking forward to a " civilised " meal, after living for three days on tinned provisions and oddments, not to speak of rusty water. Accordingly we set off for the Danish Yacht Club where by courtesy most foreign yachtsmen are allowed to dine.

We landed at the steps of the yacht basin and walked along the Langelinie. This famous walk, which runs along the harbour, and is backed by a park, was looking its best on that sunny Saturday evening. The harbour was alive with yachts, motor boats, and ferries; the basin ablaze with flags and sails; and the path itself crowded with people taking their evening walk. A few steps brought us to the Club. We needed both provisions and charts as well as the immediate necessity of food; and, knowing the shops were shutting for the week-end, we hoped the Secretary would be able to help us. The hospitality of the Danes is known the world over, and in 1923 I had received a considerable amount of assistance from the Royal Danish Yacht Club.

The Secretary, on our arrival, at once produced some excellent large-scale charts of Lim Fiord, through which we proposed to sail to the North Sea instead of being towed through the uninspiring Kiel Canal. The entrance of the

Lim Fiord both at the North Sea and Baltic Sea ends is rather difficult, so we thought ourselves fortunate in being able to obtain the Danish charts. The Secretary then sent a man out to get the beer and provisions we needed, and introduced us to Mr. Gerhard Ronne, Denmark's leading cruising man. Mr. Ronne had just returned in his five-tonner *Runa* from a cruise to Finland and Stockholm; so, apart from the pleasure in meeting another sailing man, we had a lot in common to talk over. He had also cruised to Belgium, France and England.

We had dinner in the famous dining-room upstairs. It is round in shape and has a polished wood ceiling divided into the points of the compass. The outer wall overlooking the Sound is made up of a number of large windows. It was night by then, and we sat at a table where we could look down on the Langelinie and over the harbour with its constant moving lights, and over the mass of indistinct masts, past the blurred outline of a fort into the mysterious distance of the Sound. It was blowing very hard, and even in the security of the large building we could hear the swish of vicious little harbour waves and see the riding lamps dancing. Music from the restaurant below came faintly to our ears. To us, tired mariners as we were, it was something like heaven to be in such luxury.

Dinner arrived. I forget what it was, but the memory will never be forgotten ; and I know we disgraced our country by devouring every scrap that was offered. For some days our sleep had been limited, our food had been neither nourishing nor appetising, and the labour of cooking and washing up had fallen on us; so the sudden change from hardship to luxury was almost intoxicating, and, when the time came to return to our ship, we found the utmost difficulty in walking straight across the room. The place seemed to be moving, and I sincerely trust the members who were dining at other tables had observed we had only drunk a glass of beer, a cup of coffee, and one solitary liqueur each.

Once in the open air the feeling was even worse, so that we rolled down the Langelinie arm-in-arm to the boat. The Secretary sent their man down with the provisions, and we embarked in the dinghy. For some reason this was quite a quarter full of water, and when we had rowed out of the yacht basin into the choppy water of the more open harbour, there seemed some risk of sinking. Tugs and ferries passed frequently and the bows of the dinghy seemed hardly capable of rising to their wash. It was blowing " great guns," and the smaller yachts were pitching violently. We edged into the wind, keeping always close to some yacht or other when we saw a wash approaching, in case our dinghy should sink. We had but a hundred yards to row through the anchorage, but in the difficult conditions it took quite a quarter of an hour; and we were glad when we had *Annette's* stout decks once more under our feet.

OFF MARSTAL

SAILING THE SOUND AND NORTHWARD BOUND

CHAPTER VII

DANISH SEAMEN—A FLASHING SEA AND A SPANKING BREEZE—
COASTING ZEALAND—RAIN—HUNDESTED—A VOYAGE IN-
LAND—TWO LUNATICS—HELLEROD—THE CASTLE—
FREDERIKSBORG GARDENS

ALL night it blew an easterly gale; and *Annette* rolled and pitched so that it was impossible to sleep, and we were glad, too, when morning came.

It was still blowing hard then, but the sky was clear and blue. It took time to put our shore clothes away and get the ship ready for a buffeting. By and by other yachts started to leave harbour, and the scene was further brightened up by the heightened sun on the sails and flags. Cruising yachts, racing yachts, sailing boats and motor boats slipped past two or three at a time. It was a fine Sunday, and the Dane will never miss an opportunity to be on the water. We were under way at 10 a.m. and in a few minutes were free from harbour and into the Sound, where the yachts, large and small, were circling about in readiness for racing.

We were struck with the pluck of these Danish sailors. It was blowing so hard that I had to lower our mizzen, yet these little racing craft were cutting their way with little concern in what to them must have been a great sea. Spray was driving over their crews, and in the squalls many of the

89

boats must have been really hard pressed. There is no doubt that the Danes can hold their own with any country as far as sailing is concerned; and this came as a surprise to us, accustomed as we were to meeting yachts in foreign waters only in the most settled weather. We were told that the Swedes are also fine sailors, but, not having had the opportunity of visiting either Stockholm or Goteborg, we did not come across many Swedish yachts.

We were northward bound and the racing boats were soon left behind. The coast of Denmark, smiling in the sun, lay close to port, and about five miles to starboard Sweden broke the horizon. We were approaching the island of Hven which is one of the highest in the Baltic. The waves were getting larger as the Sound widened and the sea had a longer scope in which to get up. It was cold, and the beam seas continually thrashed us with spray. Ships came past constantly and a little two-ton yacht worried her way after us. Hven gradually came abeam, the sea eased as we passed under the lee of its green-patched cliffs, and then became choppy again as we left the island astern. The Sound was becoming narrow. Elsinore of Denmark and Helsingborg of Sweden came into sight facing each other. It was grand work sailing in the flashing blue sea with a spanking breeze to urge the ship forward.

At 1 p.m. the castle of Kronborg, which guards the narrowest point of the Sound, lay on the port beam with the sun painting its walls and ramparts gold, and lightening its green turrets. We should have liked to stop there to see what enterprising guides persuade innocent tourists into believing is the grave of Hamlet; but a fair wind was with us and *Annette* foamed forward for England bound.

We had a simple lunch, and altered course slightly, leaving the Swedish coast and closing with the Danish. Gilbierg Head was soon abeam, and a heavy sea ran over some shoal ground. Once more the ship altered course and the sheets ran out to a following wind. *Annette* foamed westward along the northern coast of Zealand.

The cliffs to port rose high and fell low; houses appeared and disappeared; a wood came in view and was left astern. Thus watch by watch the afternoon slipped by, and as evening drew on *Annette* reached into the narrow entrance of Ise Fiord, until in shelter of the land. The first anchor roared out to its chain ; the second fell growling as its heavier chain rasped over the leads, and the ship lay head to wind anchored in security.

On waking next morning, August 24th, I heard the whistle of the wind in the rigging and the pattering of rain on the decks. The cabin looked damp, cold and uninviting. From the warmth of my bunk I admonished the crew to arise and get breakfast. No result. Clearly this was insubordination, so I raised my voice once again saying it was getting late. Something, which the crew denies was a muttered oath, came from the opposite bunk, and I realised that insubordination had gone to the extent of mutiny. The wind was fair, but the crew was evidently tired out, and greeted every proposal to sail with hostility. The strain of the past days had been very considerable for the "crew" as she had had little sleep for four consecutive nights.

Some people think it was wrong of me to have taken my wife on such a cruise, but such an opinion is rather narrow. It is true that the risk, the lack of sleep, the poor food and the general strain were shared by the "crew"; but she came of her own free will; she enjoyed the cruise and now looks forward to the time when we can go on another. The truth is that in the minds of some the taking of a risk is criminal and the life of a rat in a cage is considered a fitting ideal.

I had learnt that to miss a fair wind under any circumstances is most undesirable, and is not kindness to the crew. With a following wind one can run off sixty miles in daylight with the greatest ease, whereas to beat the same distance to windward may mean remaining in harbour for some days waiting for the wind to moderate, and then forty-eight hours of slow but wet and cold tacking. We argued for a short time, and it became clear that the crew was very tired indeed; and, as the next run up to Lim Fiord would involve a sail of over a hundred miles, ending with making a difficult port on a lee shore in what threatened to be half a gale of wind, we decided to remain where we were. I was also really only too glad of the excuse for a rest.

In our cruise it happened similarly, more than once, that our energy was worn out in calms and head winds, so that when a fair wind came we were too tired to enjoy it; and in this case, for example, too weary to use it at all.

There was a little village and harbour a couple of hundred yards east of our anchorage and towards midday we decided to get into port. It was raining hard and it was miserable work getting up the anchors, one of which weighed 80 lbs. and had $\frac{1}{2}$-inch a chain, and the other weighed 60 lbs. and had $\frac{5}{16}$-inch chain. *Annette* had a capstan, but the barrel was shiny and had no grooves so that it could not grip chain and could be used for rope only. Sometimes I found the anchor work very heavy and, on that day, with half a gale blowing, it was particularly hard, although the water was shallow. Just as sail was made, an extra heavy rain storm poured down on us with most depressing effect, but fortunately we had no difficulty in getting into the harbour, and in a quarter of an hour were securely moored alongside a wharf.

After changing our clothes we set out along the quay. We had brought up in the outer harbour as the inner harbour was reserved, by smell if not by law, for the fishing boats. Hundested, for that was the name of the village, is one of the chief ports of the herring industry and has a large fishing fleet. These vessels are of varying size, but most appear to be of about twenty tons. Their sail area is small, and they are propelled by very powerful paraffin engines. Unlike our English fishing boats they are painted white. At the time when we were at Hundested most of the fleet was in port, for when the wind is easterly they cannot fish. The men at that time were not very cheerful about the industry, as the Danish kroner had recently appreciated about twenty per cent to the pound. This naturally prevented the fishermen being able to sell their catch so advantageously to England and America as in former times.

We walked up the little village street which looked very clean, and the houses, with their red tiled roofs and white-washed walls, somewhat resembled dolls' houses. The hotel we found facing the shore of the fiord, and the waiter, much to our relief, could speak English. He told us that before we went we must visit the castle at Hellerod, and we agreed with him that the afternoon might be well spent in seeing something of inland Denmark. We paid our bill to which was added ten per cent for " Skat." This does not mean ten per cent for the waiter as it does in Germany, but is a State tax.

In the afternoon we caught a train of miniature and antiquated appearance for Hellerod. We travelled third class, but found it quite comfortable. Our fellow-passengers were uninteresting to us, although, on the other hand, the sound of our English appeared to surprise them. Opposite us sat a man who was extremely self-conscious because I laughed at something, and he appeared to think that he was the object of my amusement. Although there were seats vacant, a woman, with loose hair, and a home-made hat of peculiar construction ending with a tassel, insisted on standing in the corridor. She was not quite sane; and, curiously enough, on our way back the same night we encountered another lunatic. On that occasion it was a pale, fat young man who spent his time humming, adjusting his tie, peering out of the window, walking to and fro and hanging his stick in the door handle where the vibrations of the train made it continually fall down. Two lunatics encountered in our only inland journey in Denmark was a good score, but I do not suggest that it makes any reflection on the character of the Danes.

The scenery was quietly rural, and except that the line occasionally skirted the shores of Ise Fiord, the journey was dull and we were glad to get to Hellerod.

We found our way without any difficulty to the castle, Frederiksborg Slot. It is a very fine edifice surrounded by moats and a lake, and can be viewed to advantage from the town, where the lake in front and the forest as a background give it a beautiful setting ; the illustration shows it from that position. Whether the photograph is worth the trouble we had to obtain it is doubtful. We came by it as follows : We saw some photographs in a shop and entered, but nobody there could understand English, and my endeavours to explain by signs that I would buy one, provided that I was given permission to reproduce it in a book, were without success. I pointed to myself and scribbled with a pencil on a blank piece of paper. I then drew a square in which I wrote " Frederiksborg Slot," and indicated the photo, and then pointed out the word " copyright " in the dictionary. Many were the signs I made, but the only results were that first a book on photography was offered for sale, and next a scrap book. The man behind the counter became excited and shouted at his son, and passed questions with other customers. Undoubtedly I was earning my countrymen a reputation as " mad English," but I persisted until at length a neighbouring shopkeeper's wife arrived on the scene. She spoke American, and understood us without difficulty, and the photographer willingly signed the back of the photo giving me the right to have it reproduced.

But to return to Frederiksborg Slot. We walked past the outer towers, crossed a bridge over the moat and came upon the entrance which, with the porter's lodge, bore a slight resemblance to a Cambridge college. We found ourselves facing an open courtyard in which was the famous Neptune fountain; or, to be more accurate, the reproduction of the original which was carried off by the Swedes over two hundred years ago. We walked past this, out of the southern entrance, and along a box-hedged path. My recollections of all but the general impression of the castle and its beautiful surroundings are rather vague, but I remember that we walked past a lake and then along a wide road through a thick forest.

A turn to the right took us into the Frederiksborg gardens, where a restaurant reminded us of the more material want of food. Near the hotel were two very long tables at which a somewhat unusual looking lot of people were seated drinking beer. The one nearer where we sat down was occupied by men, but by men of very varying position; for some looked young and prosperous, whilst others appeared both old and needy. The other table was occupied by a number of very old women attired in black and wearing black bonnets. The waiter, who spoke English, explained that an annual event was in progress when the merchants of Hellerod took out the old-age pensioners for a drive round the town and castle, finishing in the gardens where all refreshed themselves with beer.

The season was over and, but for the old-age pensioners, who soon departed, we were the only customers of the restaurant. Dinner was very poor indeed, being clearly composed of tinned provisions, with which we were both familiar and tired.

It was dark when we left, and it would be difficult to imagine a better scene for a novelist's plot than the gardens of Frederiksborg and their surroundings. Everything was silent as we walked down the hill between the thick woods and came to the lake. There, behind the slight light that always clings round water, we saw the massive pile of the old castle with its towers stabbing up into the obscurity of the night. We crossed a moat and passed through the dim courtyards without meeting a soul.

From this old-world scene we soon found our way to the new and singularly unpleasing structure of the station. Our train proved to be electric, which for a time caused us much anxiety as, having come by a steam train, we could not reconcile ourselves to returning under any other motive force.   Moreover, none of the other passengers could speak English and their worried expressions on being questioned did nothing to allay our fears.   All went well, however, and, with the exception of the antics of the lunatic mentioned before, we had a very eventless journey, and stumbled back along the dark quays to our ship before the clock had struck eleven.

A CLEAR NIGHT

CHAPTER VIII

HELD UP BY THE "SMELLY MONSTER" AGAIN—NIGHT
SAILING—SEJRÖ ISLAND AT DAWN—A SHORT EX-
PEDITION—MORE NIGHT SAILING—LOST AT SEA

SOME yachtsmen refer to their vessels as "auxiliary sailing ships." This presumably is meant as a compliment. Now, *Annette* fell into the category of an auxiliary sailing ship, and it must be admitted that, in common with many others, I took a pride in her motor. But it was a pride entirely different to that felt by most motor yachtsmen; for I was proud, not of the efficiency of the "smelly monster," but of the number of miles I had succeeded in gaining in spite of its plots and plans. The motor was heavy, it wasted valuable room, it smelt, it caused the sails to be reduced in area on the understanding that its help could be relied upon in light winds; and above all it gave the compass deviation and annoyed the crew.

We had missed one day's fair wind through weariness which was excusable, but we were also fated to miss the following day's east wind through the "smelly monster's" obstinacy, which was damnable. To give the reader the force of the argument, I must explain that the next day we got an engineer to look at the motor. He started repairs, and we agreed to give him until midday to effect them, but, in the end, it befell that the whole "smelly monster" had to be lifted out of the ship, and carried off to the sty where other engines were under examination. This involved more delay, but although we were righteously indignant, we were not altogether sorry, for it meant another day at Hundested. The harbour there is good; and we were left to ourselves, which is rarely the case in foreign ports, for our total number of visitors only amounted to two men who came for a chat.

Although the people of Hundested took little interest in us, they were far from being uncivil. The engineer, for example, a very big fair-haired Dane whose quite effective knowledge of English had been picked up at school, was a very good fellow, and his charges were moderate. Ise Fiord is attractive and, on the last evening at Hundested, we had a very jolly walk—in the rain—along its shallow sandy shore.

Next day, August 26th, the wind was north-east, but moderate, and by 3.30 the "smelly monster" had returned to its den under the companion steps, and was reported to be in a well-disciplined condition. No sooner were we outside the harbour than the wind backed to the north-west, and, as that was almost a head wind, and the sea running was by no means small, *Annette* was not able to make very good progress.

The course lay across a slight bay, and we did not come close to the coast the other side before nightfall. On the land there was nothing conspicuous beyond an occasional windmill; for it was really but a spit some miles in length, but only a few hundred yards across. At the end of the spit ran a long reef of sand for some miles seaward, and terminated by a lighthouse. As the crow flies our destination of Sejrö Island was but a little distance from Hundested, but by sea it was about three times as far. All hope of making our objective before early morning was soon abandoned, and at 9 p.m. I took the night watch. The ship sailed on, and owing to the uncertainty of the wind the lighthouse was not brought abeam before midnight; and, as distances are so deceptive in darkness, I gave the reef a very wide berth, sailing *Annette* right out until the line of passing lights of ships indicated the deep fairway. *Annette* then lay to the west with a hint of south in her course, and a nice little breeze fanned her on her way. The weather was perfect, and a clear white moon lightened the sky and flashed on the waves. It was wonderful work steering through the sea under such perfect conditions. A faint red glow on the foresail indicated the port light was burning well, a crack of light shone through the doors to the cabin, and the binnacle lamp shed a doubtful glimmer on the compass. My mind travelled and, what with the steady motion of the ship, the musical hiss of the waves, and the fresh cold air on my face, it was extremely difficult to keep awake. Time after time the ship left her course and the helm slipped loose in my listless hand. Each time I awoke quickly as the breeze came into my face from ahead instead of abeam, and I swung *Annette's* bow back to the west; but each little time of unconsciousness exceeded in length that of its predecessor. At 2.30 a.m. I could keep awake no longer, and the crew took watch whilst the skipper slept.

When I next looked out on deck a dark mass stood picked out by the moon and a light flashed from its summit. Grey slowly displaced the blue of night and the sky astern became barred with distant red cloud. The wind was lightening; and at 6.30 a.m. the crew called me on deck;

the anchor dropped; and *Annette* lay, with sails scandalised, under the lee of the island of Sejrö. Both skipper and crew turned in for a rest after a quick but excellent breakfast.

Sejrö, as shown by the chart, is but a few miles long and is very narrow, but it is inhabited, as is the case of almost every little islet in Denmark. There is a harbour on the west side, but it is of such small importance that few ships visit it, and it is probable that before our arrival it had never been the object of a visit by a British yacht. Viewed from *Annette's* deck the island appeared most romantic. A cruel reef of rocks, which goaded a long swell into a fury of flashing white, ran in a northward direction. Sejrö at that end was quite high and a white lighthouse stood on the hill. Nearer us were a few little farmsteads; but just opposite us the coast looked wilder, and the shore was fringed by boulders in front of tumbledown cliffs. The one village lay perhaps a couple of miles to the south.

By 1 p.m. we were ready to go ashore and the dinghy was launched. A strong current was running, and the distance proved to be more than we had thought, so that I was glad when the row was over and the land was close; for sculling a diminutive dinghy is always uncomfortable work. The water was moderately deep close in, and we might safely have brought the yacht herself within fifty yards of the shore. The sea, as elsewhere in the Baltic, was remarkably transparent, and its bed could be clearly seen from the dinghy and even from *Annette*, far out as she was anchored. It was sandy, with occasional patches of weed which increased both in size and number towards the shore. Several times we caught glimpses of fish of one or two feet in length ; but we did not know to what species they belonged.

A few yards before dry land was reached the dinghy struck some of the yellow boulders which edged the island, and we had to wade ashore.

On landing we at once set off inland. The country was very pretty, but on near approach lost the wild appearance that it possessed when viewed from seaward. Far from being barren, every inch of ground was cultivated or occupied by cows, horses, sheep, geese or fowls. We strode over a miniature hill and came on a farmstead where a dog gave us an anything but friendly welcome. A track led off from this towards the village and we started to follow it. The sky was blue, there was not a breath of wind, and we found walking very hot and thirsty work, so that when we had covered a quarter of a mile we had had enough of it, and set back across country for the coast. I may add that in Denmark the traveller need have no fear of being pecked by geese or butted by either goat or cow ; for most live-stock are tethered up !

It seemed hard to have to do any work on such a hot and jolly day, but we were already far behind time, so at three o'clock the " smelly monster " was induced to raise its roar and break the silence. There was no wind, but a port lay only sixteen miles to the east. The reader will have already realised that we had abandoned the idea of sailing through Lim Fiord to the North Sea. This was because of the delay of Hundested, coupled with the fact that the wind had backed to the north. We had very much wanted to see something of North Jutland and, moreover, did not want to have the trouble of going through the Kiel Canal ; so it was a disappointment to find ourselves compelled to give up the idea of sailing north.

Hour after hour slipped by as the ship slowly made her

way across the sea between the two islands. The weather seemed to be changing and a grey mass of cloud blocked out the sky in the west. Presently a light southerly wind helped *Annette* on her course ; and the "smelly monster" was packed away. In the evening the light of Hatter Barn came abeam, marking a shoal to the north ; and a low line of hills, that indicated the island of Samsö, lay but eight miles ahead.

The helm was lashed and the ship left to sail herself whilst we, her crew, repaired below for dinner. We did not hurry, as an occasional glance at the compass showed *Annette* was holding her course ; and we relied on being able to pick out the village of Ballen through the glasses before dark.

Towards the end of the meal the ketch suddenly heeled to a fresher breeze and a patter as of rain fell on the deck, I hastened out, but quickly returned to the cabin for my oilskins, as there was a thick rain squall. *Annette* lashed forward under its weight ; but every mark, every sign of land, was completely obliterated ; and in all directions little hillocks of forlorn grey water heaved and tumbled.

The island of Samsö, however, was not far off, and I calculated that within an hour we should have the light of Ballen in sight, for *Annette* was then sailing fast. Off Sejrö a strong current had been running to the south, and accordingly I allowed for this and laid a course more to the north.

Night came on and with it heavier rain. Minutes slipped by and the time when land should be close came nearer ; and nearer ; until it had arrived.

Skipper and crew strained their eyes into the murk, but ahead no light showed a guiding beam. Away on our port quarter the powerful flash of Reef Ness marked the end of the main island ; and the Hatter Barn flashed astern, and Sejrö in the distance. *Annette* forged steadily forward. Minutes passed and I began to take soundings. It was intensely dark. Presently the crew shouted she saw something, and sure enough a fixed light appeared ahead. Then some other fixed lights, and the occasional flash in the sky of some very distant and very powerful light. The lead sounded two fathoms and we knew we were close to the coast. But there was no sign of Ballen ; the fixed lights were houses certainly, but they might have belonged to any little homestead on the coast.

We hove-to on the starboard tack, which would have kept us in deep water, but shortly after midnight the wind shifted to the west and for a time we sailed south-west. Then we came to the conclusion that we must have underestimated the southerly current, as we came about, and sailed north-west. It was pitch black in every direction with not a hint of light to differentiate between sky and land and sea. We knew the coast must be close, so we kept the lead going constantly. After some time had elapsed without anything coming into sight we again came about on the other tack, working in under the land. Very shortly after that we heard a sound of breakers and the lead recorded only four fathoms.

We fell off once more to the north and were soon in deeper water, and in confirmation of our impression that harbour lay in that direction we dimly made out a light. On we sailed, but no harbour lights came into view and suddenly we became aware that most of the lights had vanished, although a flash that presumably was Hatter Barn seemed quite near. The waves appeared to be breaking and a distant roar of breaking water became audible. I took a sounding.

It read one and a half fathoms.

We at once bore to the east, but the sea got no deeper. There was but one course of action open to us. We did not know on which side the danger lay; we did not know where to sail for safety, but nine feet of water lay below us. Down went the foresail, and in two minutes *Annette* lay to her anchor by ten fathoms of rope.

We were lost, utterly lost; and every attempt at plotting the position on the chart proved the inaccuracy of our calculations. Even allowing for an error of considerable amount there seemed on the chart to be no patch of shallow water near the Hatter Barn, or between it and the mainland. We gave up the problem and rested, whilst *Annette*, between the forces of a strong current and the wind, rolled and pitched in the darkness. The wind was by this time off the island of Samsö, but the waves were large enough to prove no land could be within a couple of miles to windward, so we were anchored on some sea-bound sandy shoal.

The night passed slowly, but sleep was impossible owing to the motion of the ship. At last the indefinite light of dawn in dirty weather tinged the waves grey, and patches of land gradually took shape. With day came wonder, simple wonder, for when we had last seen solid ground it had been the distant regular shore of Samsö, and that was what we had expected.

Instead, however, of the scene we had imagined and counted on, there arose an utterly different picture of sea and land. Quite close to the south-west the gaunt pile of some small rocky island rose sheer from the sea. Nearer lay some low ground which appeared to be connected with the mainland that swept round in a curve from the west to the north, leaving the bay in which *Annette* had rolled so miserably all the previous night.

It was a most unreal awakening, and a look at the chart in no way lessened the problem. The sail of some fishing or trading boat presently came into sight, so I quickly raised anchor, and *Annette* followed the strange craft. I kept the lead going and the sea presently deepened and, as the sky grew lighter and the configuration of the coast clearer, an idea crossed my mind. I looked once more at the chart, but at a position some fifteen miles north of our calculation. The coast line shown agreed with that in front of us. To make sure I gave the chart to the crew who unhesitatingly came to the same conclusion. To make matters absolutely certain the vessel ahead altered course and we saw two beacons which we found marked on the chart.

It may be difficult for the landsman to appreciate the wonder of our position. The yacht during the night had steered herself through a narrow channel between two islands; she had chosen the one right path through a maze of shallows, rocks and islands.

Having ascertained our position, it was a matter of no great difficulty to sail back to Ballen. For the greater part of an hour *Annette* sailed south-east towards the gaunt islet of Sejrö, keeping well off another island to starboard from which a long patch of rocks ran out. Then she altered course and lay south through the narrow channel between the two reefs projecting from each island. A strong current ran against us and we heard a sound of breaking water similar to that observed in the dark hours of the previous night, leaving no doubt that that was the channel that we had navigated.

We were very cold and tired, but we felt much better after a warm meal cooked by the crew. The ship was sailing fast, and before ten o'clock two piers came into view that marked the missing harbour of Ballen; and shortly afterwards we anchored under the weather shore of the island of Samsö.

EVENING FALLS

CHAPTER IX

A DANISH INN——DANISH HOSPITALITY——CRUISING IN COMPANY
——EBELTOFT FOLKLORE——THE NORWEGIANS——GROWING A
SHIP——FARMERS AT SEA

BALLEN is a most picturesque little harbour. Two piers, gradually curving towards each other, form the outer breakwaters, and between these, but further in, is a third pier. This encloses on the one hand a wide sheet of water terminating and gradually shallowing to a sandy shore; and, on the other hand, a narrow neck of water connecting with two or three little basins in which lie a few trading vessels and fishing boats.

It was at about midday when we rowed past the quaint old quays and landed on the road facing the sea. An hotel faced us and towards this we made a bee line. There did not seem to be a soul about, but in the dining-room we saw the remains of a most unappetising looking meal, and we found a bell which, after a few rings, produced a servant. She could not understand English, but we had not any difficulty in explaining our wants and she disappeared in a hurry, feeling it an urgent matter to supply the English with food before they fell dead from privation in her dining-room. A bad advertisement for the inn, that would be.

The remains of the meal were cleared away from the

table, and presently returned in a re-heated condition; and, as an example of Danish country food, it is worthy of description. It consisted of two courses only. The first was a pink-coloured soup of plum apple and sago, with one solitary house fly by way of flavouring; the second, of some very highly flavoured black sausages and, what was more palatable, a dish of potatoes boiled in their skins. As might have been expected, the charge for the meal was modest.

After lunch we wandered round the village looking for shops; and in the evening we sailed *Annette* into the harbour and berthed alongside a wharf, where the harbour-master introduced himself in order to collect the dues and a drink. The latter gift was perhaps unwise, for it soon appeared that he had already fortified himself with alcohol before coming to see us; but the drop of Scotch whisky set his tongue wagging and also endowed him with a wonderful sense of humour. It seemed to amuse him that we were sailing alone, and he kept on repeating in English of extraordinarily poor quality, " two of you! "; and then he would emit a cracked, quavering chuckle. Whatever I said seemed to be very funny; so we were not altogether sorry when he departed to clamber his way back along the rough boulders which formed the quay.

The most striking thing about Ballen is its hospitality to strangers. The ship chandler's was run by an elderly and well-educated lady. She was most businesslike but, after we had paid the bill for the provisions, she took us over to her fruit garden which she claimed to be one of the oldest on the island. It was shady and pretty, and was obviously the delight of her heart. She gave us some pears and then took us to her vegetable garden and gave us a selection for a salad. In a similar hospitable way the people of the farm, where we went for milk, asked us into their private room for a talk ; but in that case the motive was perhaps not quite so disinterested, for I fancy their real motive was to test the quality of their daughter's English.

We went for a walk along a road leading inland and found the country quietly attractive and remarkably free from the curse of motor cars.

Of the people we met hardly one failed to nod or imply " good evening." On our return to the ship, as we passed along the quay, we saw a little half-decked yacht had entered, and her owner and his wife were busy baling her out. She had come from Fredericia and was really very full of water indeed. As it had been blowing remarkably hard during the day we were forced again to admit what very fine sportsmen are the Danes.

Shortly afterwards another yacht entered, but she was a considerable contrast to the other Danish boat, being a great ketch of about twenty tons. As soon as things were coiled down her owners went ashore and at once came to ask us aboard for coffee, an invitation which we accepted as soon as we had finished our dinner.

The complement of the *Amfitrite*, as the new-comer was named, consisted of the owner, a doctor friend and his son, daughter and niece; whilst forward two sea scouts comprised the crew. The owner, Mr. J——sen, and his Swedish friend Dr. G——, were oldish men of the type that can make one feel quickly at home ; and in a few minutes we all knew each other. Mr. J——sen told us about his home at Aarhus; and explained that he was a ship chandler who had started in quite a small way and had picked up his English and education in the school of practical experience. The doctor, too, had led an interesting life, having served his time in the American navy in China during his younger days. He had but recently qualified in medicine, and claimed to have taken his degree later in life than almost anybody in Sweden. The favourite medicine he advised was a sort of white corn brandy, the Danish national drink, which he offered us liberally.

That evening in Ballen will not easily be forgotten ; for, after what seemed months of voyaging in foreign waters, we were amongst friends. Everybody spoke natur-ally ; and I suppose there is no place in the world that can compare to a ship's cabin for cosiness. The two Danes off the little yacht were guests like ourselves, but they did not speak English and I felt afterwards that it was rather rude of us to have monopolised conversation. We learnt to our surprise that they had intended to sleep on their little craft until Mr. J——sen offered them a cabin ; and, for the second time, I mentally raised my hat to them—for their craft had but two or three feet headroom, and we saw with our own eyes that everything aboard was soaked through.

Next morning we went to breakfast on the *Amfitrite*; as her owners had decided that it was their duty to play the part of hosts to the other smaller yachts.

The owners of the little racing yacht departed directly after breakfast, and we went to the end of the pier to give them a send off.

The wind was almost southerly and so, as it was no use to make towards Kiel, we decided to sail north-west to Aarhus in company with *Amfitrite*. *Annette* being the slower of the two was the first to get under way. The scouts carried a line across to the opposite pier so that we might haul off from our position where the wind pinned us alongside the quay. The harbour-master boarded us and, with his cackling laugh, assisted in pulling away at the rope. I had to shout three times to get him to desist and, by the time he let go, *Annette* was quite close to the weather pier; but there still seemed room to swing round, although not as much as I should have liked. The harbour-master was talking rapidly and incoherently, and starting to lower my sails. He was not merely a noisy nuisance, but a positive menace to the ship's safety, so I showed him the way to his dinghy where he stood up, still talking very fast and gesticulating.

The mizzen and jib had been set, and I went forward and loosened the rope leading to the pier. The jib filled and the bow fell off, whilst I held on to the rope at the same time walking towards the stern, to ensure that *Annette* should fall off sufficiently. " Let go ! " yelled the harbour-master ; and I was fool enough involuntarily to obey him. The yacht gathered way but, instead of falling off further and shaping out to sea, she tended to come closer to the wind. My wife shouted, and I dashed aft to clear the mizzen sheet which had doubled itself under the curve of the horse. Too late! There was a heavy crash and the bowsprit ran in between two piles of the pier. One of the large round boulders, of which the mole was built, was lifted bodily up into the air by the impact, until I thought it must topple over into the sea the other side.

I dashed forward, pushed the yacht's head off, and we sailed out seawards. The bowsprit was broken but hanging together by a few splinters, and I broke it right off with my hands, and, as a parting gift, I threw it back on to the end of the pier as we passed.

The damage to the ship was negligible for we rarely

used the bowsprit, and, in any case, the spar was but a cheap ill-finished makeshift. The damage to our pride was much more serious, for our Danish friends had assembled to give us a cheer off. We felt very foolish indeed, although the accident was mainly due to the harbour-master, who had insisted on hauling us too close to the weather pier. On several previous occasions I have got into trouble through the unwanted assistance of harbour loafers anxious for a tip, but this time money had been refused and as the motive was kindness I could not curse him to my heart's content. Whilst I do not share the hackneyed opinion that the words "well meant" convey the deepest of insults, it seems to me that good intentions which cause trouble are infinitely more irritating. One can put up with meanness, for example, and even enjoy making jokes about it ; but who can tolerate the person who, having beguiled one to tea, presses one to stay on for dinner as well ?

Once outside Ballen we lay to and hoisted sail properly. Our course was back in the tracks of where we had sailed the previous day. The *Amfitrite* soon followed out of the harbour and rapidly gained on us, passing *Annette* as she entered the channel between Vejrö Island and the other islets. It blew very hard and, when in the afternoon we had cleared the island of Samsö and sailed past the long reef projecting from its northern extremity into the more open water, the sea was rough although not dangerous, as the wind had but eight miles in which to lash it up. The hard breeze had shifted to north-west, and once in the choppy water, *Annette* seemed to be able to hold the *Amfitrite* in speed. But when the latter had crossed the dividing sea and got close to the Jutland coast she altered course and ran east, gaining rapidly. We realised that they had found the weather too bad to allow them to beat west to Aarhus, and we quite agreed with their decision, for it would have been a wet, cold, and tiring sail. What was happening to the little yacht bound for Hundested was a serious thought that crossed our minds. She had a following wind, but the sea was very rough for so small a boat. Two months later we heard that they had managed to make harbour safely.

It was not long before the shelter of a great open bay was gained, and we foamed along in smooth water. The sun was out and the coast exceedingly pretty, being higher than elsewhere in Denmark, and consisting of undulating fields running down to the water's edge.

We followed the Danish yacht into the harbour of Ebeltoft at 4 p.m.; and, having anchored and roughly coiled down, went aboard *Amfitrite* for a meal. Our friends agreed with us that *Annette* was a remarkably fine sea boat, for she had carried full sail, and had experienced little discomfort, whereas the great twenty-tonner had received quite a dusting, in spite of having stowed her mizzen and only having carried reefed mainsail and storm jib.

Ebeltoft is not very often visited by English people, for it is not easy to find, being tucked away in a peninsula; but it is one of the oldest and most interesting towns of Denmark. We set out to see the place the next day, Sunday, as it was blowing a full gale and sailing was out of the question.

On landing, the first curious thing that meets the eye is the sea-wall. This is composed entirely of seaweed, and is over four hundred years old. The labour required to build it must have been prodigious, for seaweed shrivels up to very small bulk when dried ; and the wall was built of the compressed weed. One of the "show places" of the village is the dye works, which is many hundred years old. It did not interest us so much as some of the quaint little courtyards and leafy gardens which are to be found in the town. The main street is neither particularly pretty nor unusual, beyond the fact that many of the houses are white-washed and have but one storey. The bakers' shops, as elsewhere in Denmark, are marked by a curly golden sign representing a twist but looking from a distance not unlike a crown. The clean exterior of a Danish baker's, with its rows of beautiful cakes, often attracts the traveller sufficiently to make him purchase what he does not want. Several times in Denmark we went into one of these shops for coffee and cakes; but although the former was extremely good, the latter invariably proved a disappointment: being very rich and much too creamy, or more often than not sub-merged by a mass of cold sticky custard.

The best-known building in Ebeltoft, I suppose, is its old courthouse. It is now a museum, and we looked over the place. Down below are some particularly damp and gruesome dungeons, but the pride of the place seems to lie in the fact that a witch was sentenced there to be burnt to death. She avoided the sentence by dying after torture. It did not interest us particularly, as almost every country town has had its ancestral brutes; and, if what one reads in the papers is true, our own generation is but little more civilised.

More amusing was a book we bought on the Men of Mols, the district in which Ebeltoft is situated. The inhabitants of Mols have had the reputation in the past of being particularly stupid, and the book contains a collection of local tales that have been passed on from one generation to another. Mr. J——sen translated a few to me, but the humour depends greatly on the way the story is told. For example, a few pages explain how a Norwegian ship came into the harbour of Ebeltoft. One of the inhabitants, never having seen a Norwegian before, set off down to the harbour to see the skipper. He found the ship without difficulty, but her crew were below at their midday dinner, and the decks were deserted save for a basket of lobsters that had just been purchased. The Man of Mols hesitated for a long time wrapt in thought, but at last went forward and shook hands with the nearest lobster, saying, " Welcome to Ebeltoft, Mr. Norwegian! "

It is a silly story, but in the original Danish it is probably told in a more amusing way, and the illustrations in the book are good—particularly the one depicting the expression of the Molbo on finding himself pinched in the large claws of what he took to be the Norwegian skipper.

Another story relates how the Men of Mols very much wanted to have a big ship of their own. Even in those days financial questions took a position of prominence, and a meeting of the council decided they could not afford to buy anything larger than a fishing boat. Fortunately, amongst them was a philosopher, and he, being cleverer than the others, suggested that they should buy a boat from a big ship at anchor off the harbour, and wait for it to grow. This plan was immediately adopted and they set out to interview the owners of the ship; with the result that they shortly returned poorer in pocket but richer by a boat. They put their purchase in a garden to grow, but after some weeks found that, although it looked older and more weather-beaten, it had not increased in size. They then decided to take it down to the shore near its native element, and surround it with weed, on which it could feed. Many months passed and the boat still remained small, and its increased antiquity gave them no satisfaction. The philosopher was becoming by no means popular, but saved himself by suggesting that the boat would not grow unless near its " mummy "; so the next time the big ship came back they rowed out once more to interview the captain. The latter agreed to take the boat away for a sea voyage providing the Molsmen would pay for its passage. Terms were agreed, and the day came when the big ship left Ebeltoft. The boat was being towed, and jumped so much in the short seas that the philosopher remarked, " See how happy it is by its mother. See how it bounds for joy." Sad to relate, the Men of Mols are still waiting for the return of the boat, which has by now, no doubt, attained the size of a full-rigged ship.

We were told that the inhabitants of the Mols district are still far from being up to the standard of intelligence that prevails elsewhere in Denmark. As recently as in the last century two of them distinguished themselves as follows : Two farmers were bound on a little boat from Aarhus to Ebeltoft and soon after they had started it became foggy and the wind freshened. Having no compass and little experience of navigation they wisely decided to put back to where they had started. In the evening they sighted a red light, and, thinking it was the harbour light, Laus, who was acting as captain, told his partner to sail for it. The latter was somewhat uncertain as to whether he agreed with his skipper and said he could see a lot of other lights moving. "Oh," replied Laus, "those are the housewives in town moving with the lamps in their rooms, so just you do as you are told, and steer for the red! "

There was a splitting crash and they ran full into a steamer. She was the Copenhagen passenger steamer; but fortunately was going at half-speed owing to the fog. A boat was lowered and one of the men picked up and brought on deck.

" . . . dare you sail without lights or foghorn, and did you not hear my whistle ? " asked the steamer's master.

" Don't blame me," replied the man, " I am no sailor and had to obey Laus."

" Laus! Who's Laus ? " demanded the captain.

" Oh, if he is not here, he must be in the water," was the bright reply. The boat was again lowered, and Laus fortunately picked up before he was drowned.

IN THE SOUND

CHAPTER X

SOUTH'ARD BOUND—SVENDBORG SOUND—DIFFICULT NAVI-
GATION—A DASH ROUND A HARBOUR—A WHIRLING
MASS OF BLACK FOAM-FLECKED WATER—WELCOME TO
STRYNÖ—AN ISLAND DISCOVERED—GALE CONTINUES—
A DANISH COTTAGE

TO return once more to the subject of the *Amfitrite*. The doctor had important business so that he and his party left the yacht and went by train to Aarhus.

In addition to various excursions ashore we managed to carry on some small but important work. We often had to put up with a lot of trouble with *Annette's* halyards, which were too large in size to render through the blocks, with the result that occasionally we had exciting moments when the mainsail could not be lowered. Mr. J——sen arranged for the hand off a schooner, that was lying at the wharf near us, to come aboard *Annette* and reeve new halyards. We could have done the work ourselves, but such spare time as we had was valuable, and the splices of an experienced rigger were undoubtedly more to be trusted than our makeshifts.

Another point of importance was the matter of charts, for our English ones, though good in their way, were of very small scale. Mr. J——sen kindly gave me some of his own and also a copy of that admirable work, the *Danske Havne-Lods*, which shows plans of all the harbours. My crew he presented with a little gold brooch representing a Viking ship, saying that she had been unanimously elected a member of the " Viking " club, but of the exact status that the order conferred we were told nothing.

Next day the wind moderated, enabling us to sail. In the morning Mr. J——sen begged us to lay up *Annette* at Aarhus and go home by steamer, but, being unable to convince us of the wisdom of his plan, he thought that at least we should take one of his scouts as additional crew. They were good willing boys and we seriously considered his kind offer, but came to the conclusion that we could never tolerate the presence, however desirable, of a third person on board. After lunch the scouts helped me to raise anchors and make sail; and *Annette* slipped out of the harbour past the shallows, and then headed along the bay for the open sea.

The *Amfitrite*, bound for Aarhus, was to follow, but the weather was so threatening that Mr. J——sen decided to lay up his yacht where she was, and return by train, as his holiday was over.

That night we gained the harbour of Ballen, where we noticed the harbour was marked by one high light, and by small green and red lamps at the pierheads that could only be seen at comparatively close quarters.

Next day we started early, but it was soon blowing half a gale of wind, and as soon as we passed out beyond the shelter of Samsö we felt the full force of the storm. The sea was rough, but *Annette* sailed fast and soon gained the shelter of the island of Fyen. All day the yacht reached south, down the Great Belt, at a good six knots, sometimes crossing bays and sometimes coasting or passing between shoal or island. As the hours of daylight drew near their end, the weather grew wilder, and at dusk the wind was very violent; but by then we were in the sheltered water near Svendborg Sound. We decided not to carry on further to Rudkoping, as the navigation threatened to be most complicated. The chart showed a channel but a few feet in width, that followed a winding course in a large shallow sea. We had been told not to navigate this without a pilot, so it was certainly not wise to make the attempt by ourselves in darkness; and we therefore tacked west towards Svendborg.

Night soon fell on us, but the twisting Sound is clearly marked by a series of leading lights that must be kept in line. There was no difficulty in following these guides, although once we were surprised to find the channel ran very close to a spit of sand.

At about 9 p.m. we anchored under a lighthouse near a schooner. There was a strong current running, to which, once the sails were down, the ship lay comfortably. After the long day's passage we were very tired but very happy, as we had made fine progress, and the finding of shelter among the dark islands was an event full of romance.

It rained heavily during the night, and it was still blowing very hard when we turned out at 6 a.m. next morning. At eight we started under scandalised mainsail, and foamed down the channel. Buoys slipped by to port, then up went the storm jib and peak, while the yacht reeled nearer the wind and fled to the south across the fiord. Another mark appeared to port, passed in a flash, and in a few minutes a line of buoys came into sight guiding the channel to Rudkoping. Close in came the sheets and the ship's stem headed west, bringing the wooded shores of the main island abeam. White booms were left to starboard in quick succession, red to port; broom buoys to port and again cross buoys to starboard. Suddenly a large boom ornamented by a broom and a cross loomed up close ahead. Did it mark right or left-hand bank? Little time to think; for the yacht in the hard wind was putting yards of foam-flecked sea behind her every minute. The keen sight of the crew picked up a more distant boom showing red. Out ran the sheets, and two hands taut on the tiller swung *Annette* off on a more southerly course.

We were racing down some strange alley between sandbanks; but a cluster of marks away to starboard puzzled us for a moment, until suddenly we realised there must be two channels and the peculiar buoy marked the fork where they divided. All attention was called to the steering; for, with the wind abeam, the ship needed all care to coax down the narrow channel, which in many places was less than ten yards across. Minutes passed like seconds, and we found ourselves once more close hauled with the town of Rudkoping close on our own port bow. Our chart was too small and was out of date, showing no leading marks whatever. The wind was of almost gale strength and the water choppy. The sea which we were approaching was shallow, with depths varying from one to fifteen feet, and dotted with numerous shoals and several rocks. The big foresail could hardly be controlled in the squalls. Harbour was close and quick thought essential to continue safely the run for shelter.

Rudkoping came abeam, Rudkoping was past, and the waves broke aboard in flying spray as *Annette* lay closehauled to the wind. Lee-o-o!—and she came up with sails thrashing and blocks clattering their protest, as the ropes whipped the deck in fruitless rage. Helm over; and *Annette* slipped astern, fell off on the other tack; and, gathering speed, ran like a harried hare into the shelter of the harbour. It was a small harbour and seconds counted as hours. Quick, helm up ; and she ran along, passed a quay; then a quay came straight ahead and a dolphin to starboard. Close round this she sped, while every ounce of strength was thrown into hauling in the sheet. Lee-o-o!— and she was close to another quay and off on the other tack. Then once more round the dolphin, close to a steamer, and then with helm hard up she gathered speed. Hard down, and she ran alongside a quay with sails a-tremble. Down came the jib. Down the peak. A line was taken by willing hands ashore and the ship was moored.

Almost stunning to our wits we found the sudden quiet after the hiss of wind and spray, so for some time we contented ourselves with cleaning up ship. Presently we changed and went ashore, leaving the yacht to the care of the crowd assembled on the quay. Nothing would be touched, we knew, for although each individual might be dishonest taken by himself, yet as a member of the crowd he would be not only highly principled, but also willing to act as policeman. In short, what is known to the Law as " collusion " would be necessary to make any pilfering possible.

Before we had gone very far we met a courteous harbour-master, who spoke English, and he took us to a ship's chandler's, where he acted as interpreter. We bought a large-scale chart of the surrounding waters, and arranged for a new strop to be made for the peak halyards, as this had parted in one of the squalls. A skipper of a neighbouring three-masted schooner was also buying gear and he, of course, spoke English. His ship was northward bound for timber, and then back south to Cork.

Having bought all our requirements we set out to see the town; but, as time was short, we did not find much of interest beyond several very picturesque old houses. As the sum remaining to our credit on our traveller's note was running short we had lunch at a baker's shop instead of at an hotel. Danish bakers usually have a room labelled "Cafe" and "Condituri" where light refreshments may be purchased.

When we arrived back at the ship we found the man with a mizzen halyard strop ready for us; and repairs were quickly effected. In the meantime a Customs official had arrived, and my time was fully occupied between answering his questions and attending to the rigger; but he was soon satisfied that everything was in order and, after shaking hands, he departed. The harbour-master and the ship chandler then came below for a quick drink before we started.

At 3 p.m. sails were set—the storm jib and mainsail alone—and the new large-scale chart was laid on the deck securely pinned down. A crowd assembled to cheer us off, ropes were loosed and *Annette* fell off as her sails filled. The first tack took us across the harbour to the dolphin, where we came about, and the second took us back to the south quay. It was blowing a full gale and, as we came about, the violent slatting of the jib sheets made one of them part. It was rather a critical moment, for we were in very narrow space with only about fifty feet to lie on each tack. It took us three tacks to negotiate this and, more by luck than good management, we managed to beat our way out. It was most exciting work, for each board took us so close to one or other of the quays, that we were able actually to help the ship about by pushing her bows off with a boat-hook. The crew was steering and, what with the roar of the gale, and the trouble of the broken jib sheet, she played her part well in keeping her head so cool.

Annette slipped past the mouth of the harbour and, when we had secured a good offing, she was brought on to the other tack and, at the same time, I repaired the broken jib sheet. Once more the mad career started. The channel was narrow and the spray flashed from the short seas right over the ship, half blinding us. Two hands on the tiller could hardly keep the yacht steady, with the result that in the confusion we went right out of our course. The crew was at the helm, and, when we found the proper channel, she gave the steering over to me as it was beyond her physical strength, and she turned " pilot " whilst I became " crew." She quickly grasped the position and soon she navigated the ship back into the fairway, but we had to tack and, as the ship came about, the patent boom jaws slipped from the mast as the spar shook wildly about. This was dangerous on a lee shore, and for some minutes we laid back towards Rudkoping; but then, as the ship came about, I managed to slip the boom into its proper place and put a wire to replace the broken fastening. By that time we were familiar with the channel and navigation thenceforward was easy. We found that when we had been off our course the depth of water had been between five and seven feet. *Annette* drew three and a half, but as her centre plate had been half down she had probably required at least five. I knew that as shown by the chart there was water enough where we had been, but it had been anxious work, for charts are not always perfectly reliable.

Our course took us south of Strynö Island, where we were well protected from the north-west wind; but, once past the island, there lay a big expanse of sea with numerous shoals and islands, and with only a maximum depth of about fifteen feet. The average depth was not more than nine feet; and, as there were many miles in which the sea could gather with a nor'-westerly wind, a rough passage was to be expected. Our expectations were fully realised, for as we slipped from the shelter of the island, we ran into a whirling mass of black foam-broken water. *Annette*, with a gale whistling in her sails, plunged frantically into the seas. Nothing would stop her, and the waves broke over the bows ; lashed over the dinghy fastened on the foredeck; and then, in heavy blinding spray, drove furiously in our faces, whilst the heavier water careered down the deck and out of the lee scuppers. In spite of oilskins we were soon drenched; and, the wind backing to the west, made it necessary to tack. Each tack was a matter of deliberation; for it is always difficult to get a sailing ship to stay in a heavy sea, and when the ship lies head to wind there is the ever-present danger of the sails blowing away as they slat madly in the panic of the gale.

By carefully choosing smooth water between the squalls, we successfully brought off this operation three times; but then, as we were in dangerous waters which required careful navigation, and it was impossible to see the buoys through the driving spray, we decided to give up; and in a few minutes we had run back under the lee of Strynö Island. We tacked close under the shore and dropped anchor in about three-quarter fathom; but, although the jib was loose, the ship took charge under the driving force of the gale and made a dead set for the rock jetty, dragging her anchor after her as though it were a half-pound weight. I was too slow in getting the sails down, and in a minute she had ranged alongside the mass of broken stone; but the wind driving straight off shore carried her past this and, just as she was clearing the wooden end of the pier, I managed to throw a rope ashore. This was made fast, and three men jumped aboard and in a few minutes *Annette* lay alongside a trading vessel with sails furled.

Thus was an introduction formed with the inhabitants of the island of Strynö, and in particular with one named Karl. Karl was a tall energetic man of middle age; but a stranger might have credited him with sixty or more years. He came below and shook hands warmly, talking quickly in some language mixed with English. We made out that for some reason he was particularly friendly with the English, and he also conveyed his beliefs that Strynö was the best place in the world, and that *Annette* was the first English ship to have laid alongside the quay there. He took me by the arm beckoning me to follow; so that, in my shirt-sleeves and soaked to the skin, I was conducted to the warm cabin of a neighbouring schooner.

The skippers of the other craft were gathered there waiting a turn in the weather. We shook hands and then sat down to a bottle of beer and a glass of the national " Akvavit "—a spirit of exceptionally nice flavour, and very warming. One of the captains spoke English perfectly, and was able to act as interpreter between Karl and myself, much to the disgust of the latter, who prided himself on his knowledge of languages. Karl's hospitality was almost as embarrassing as enthusiastic, for he insisted on his country-men pressing me with cigars and apples. Moreover, when the butcher came on board for a drink he demanded that he should be given meat for five persons at a special price in honour of our visit; and, when this request was refused, he took off his coat and wanted to fight, until he was

quietened down by the others. After a short time my wife,
who had been changing into dry clothes, came aboard and
also partook of beer and apples. There is no country that

THE ISLAND OF STRYNÖ

can vie with Denmark for simple hospitality, and although,
perhaps, the seamen were more boisterously good-humoured
than polished, they were models of courtesy when my wife
was present.

Later on in the evening, after the cabin had been tidied up and we had eaten something more substantial than apples, we all walked up to the village, where Karl beckoned us into a shop, and asked us what we should like in memory of our visit. To make up one's mind quickly and decide on something of more sentimental than intrinsic value is by no means simple. Fortunately my wife saw a little glass vase on a shelf, and the question was solved; but when we afterwards found it was ornamented with silver we felt rather uncomfortable at having allowed him to spend so much, for at that moment Karl was one of the unemployed. After the visit to the shop we were taken to the house of the captain who spoke English. His " frou " quickly prepared coffee and brought cigars and spirits. She also brought the family postcard album, which contained a collection gathered together from all parts of the world. Amongst these, which were mostly photos and bad paintings of towns and harbours, rested one in which particular pride was taken and whose origin was represented as English. The morality of this postcard was perfect, but it would hardly have been suitable for exhibition in an English drawing-room, although the humour possibly somewhat balanced the lack of what is usually considered delicacy.

We returned to the ship at about nine-thirty. It was a wild night with the clouds racing past the moon. The wind howled down the road to the pier, and occasional spots of cold rain drove after us and hastened our way towards the ship. The sea was black, save where a silver break in the clouds allowed faint light to glimmer down on the crests of the waves. We were not a little thankful to be in harbour, for when we went below we found the barometer had dropped no less than eight-tenths in forty-eight hours, of which four-tenths had been within the last twenty-four! After a tiring day it is not pleasant to have to get up early the following morning ; but, as Karl had sworn that he was coming aboard at six to show us the church, we had perforce to be up betimes ; although, as it turned out, his lined mahogany face did not appear before seven, when he came down to breakfast. We had been told quite a lot about him by the captain, and he was really an unusual character. His father had been drowned at sea off Gotland when still middle-aged, and his mother had also died when he was young, but Karl had made his way and bought a large hotel in Copenhagen, which he kept until but three months ago, when for some reason he lost everything, and even his wife left him. Karl was one of the best, but, although he would not take more than an occasional drink with us, I fancy his failing was the popular one.

He now lived on the little island, where he eked out an uncertain existence by means of a small motor boat, which represented the remainder of his capital. He insisted on telling all his life history to us, which was no doubt a relief to him, since he had few friends and lived amid the half-humorous gibes of the islanders. He was a somewhat romantic figure in his way. There was something pleasing about his clear grey eyes and his smile, and the occasional distant dreamy look. Of course he was not normal. There was nothing, however, he would not do for us and he was constantly tending our warps, getting water and performing the many little kindnesses that can be done for a foreigner. Many times a day he used to shake hands and tell me that he had seen me at Copenhagen in 1923; but whether this was fact or fiction I cannot say.

The barometer was still falling fast but the wind was

moderate, so at nine we decided to sail. At ten we were back again, for in the thick rain we soon found that we could scarcely see two hundred yards; and the wind being southerly made it necessary to tack so frequently that it was not wise to carry on for the port, surrounded as it was by shallows. The channel between the shoals was narrow and winding and we should probably not have been able to distinguish the leading marks in the murk.

Little was left to do but the day passed in reading, writing and cleaning the cabin. In the afternoon we went ashore to see the village by daylight. First we called at the ship's chandler's for some stores. He at once asked us into the inner room, and his wife in the usual hospitable Danish way brought some excellent coffee and cakes. The little room was clean and bright—really as nice as a cottage room could be. The walls were of blue distemper with a white frieze, the ceiling of close planks supported by heavy beams enamelled white, and the floor of light oak was polished bright as a new penny. A telephone hung in a corner and a little bureau showed that business was occasionally transacted. The church was not far off, past a few houses and trees; it was not old but the tower looked as though many hundreds of years had elapsed since it had been built. Near the church lay what must be one of the most beautiful villages in Denmark.

An old farm-house fronted with a pond and a couple of golden hayricks faced us, and old houses, with beams picked out in black against the whitewash background, and crowned with heavy thatch green with age, were clustered in haphazard fashion round the open space in front of the buildings. A number of little gardens with shrubs and flowers replaced what in England would have been the village green. It was a most charming old-world spot, absolutely unknown to tourists, where the inhabitants lived simply on the produce of their land just as their fathers had before them. There was no poverty on that island; no wealth either, and perhaps that was the reason why everybody seemed so civil and friendly. Passers-by, without exception, touched their hats in the straightforward way that showed brotherly socialism had not taught them to look on strangers as enemies.

It is always pleasing to be the first to find anything new, so to be the first English people to land on the island of Strynö was in itself a great pleasure.

Our delight with the find was but a passing feeling, for it happened that the weather remained bad, and for several days we were confined to the land of our discovery. The barometer behaved in an extraordinary way, rapidly rising and then as rapidly falling, but even the upward movements of the glass did not affect the weather, which remained very bad. A succession of storms of rain and wind of winter violence passed the island. It was bitterly cold, too, but fortunately an end comes even to a gale; and on September the eighth we realised that, in spite of pessimists who predicted we should have to leave the yacht at Strynö, it was possible to sail.

SIMRISHAMN

CHAPTER XI

I HURRIED up to the grocer's for provisions, which after a very long wait I obtained. During my absence Karl had boarded *Annette* and prepared her for sea. When I arrived at the pier I found his little motor boat alongside and, in spite of my remonstrances, he insisted he was going to tow the yacht to Marstal. He also kidnapped two passengers who were about to board a steamer, offering them a free passage.

His five-horse-power engine started with a roar, ropes were cast off, and *Annette* slowly forged west in tow of the motor boat. There was a moderate head wind and I fancy Karl found his charge heavier than expected ; but he carried on cheerfully, although the two passengers that he had kidnapped (who had business in Marstal) did not appear to share his happy frame of mind. We were crossing a semi-protected sea which was safe enough for *Annette* even in a gale, but was hardly suitable in uncertain weather for an open boat like that of Karl. After half an hour the engine broke down and the wind rapidly carried us southeast, but the delay was not long enough to matter seriously. The voyage continued and Karl, much to our annoyance, gave the helm to the lady passenger, who was incapable of steering straight, and kept on turning round with a self-conscious smile as if to say, " Aren't I clever ! " Karl's navigation also was more thrilling than we should have liked. His motor boat could cross any sands, but I do not think he allowed anything for our deeper draught. Perhaps he knew the sea very well and could consequently calculate within inches over what shoals we could pass; but " I hae ma doots " and I fancy something more than skill guided Karl's optimistic course.

It took about an hour and a half to cross the sea and come near Marstal, and it was there that the difficult shoals were to be found. My crew, whose sight is very good, picked out the right channel, but our friend had no intention of following this, and his amiable passenger, assisted by her "young man," steered cheerfully in semi-circles over the sands in apparent ignorance of the danger. My crew was furious and in such a state of mutiny that I hastily hoisted sail in response to her orders. By the time we were ready to sail, *Annette* was being towed over one of the shallowest parts marked on the chart and, when I looked over the side, the sands looked as though they were but a foot or two below the surface. It was no use to cast off then, for the correct channel was a hundred yards a'starboard, and the chances were that we should run aground before getting on the right course. So we hung on with teeth set whilst the motor boat chugged sturdily ahead. In two minutes we were safely across and in the deep fairway near the shore. The wind was abeam and we were on our own. Karl, since casting us off, had cut off a corner and landed on a pier where he stood waving his hand in farewell to his English friends. Our feelings of anger at his navigation changed to gratitude, for the old fellow had been very good to us ;

his tow had saved us a lot of trouble, and the cost to him in petrol must have been material—and money perhaps that he could ill afford. We gave him the benefit of the doubt, and agreed that he had taken us through some short cut to Marstal that was not marked on the chart.

The channel lay close to the town, which has an attractive appearance when viewed from the sea. It is entirely a seafaring place, and can boast of more ships than many a seaport of twice its size. A sea captain had told us that we could not possibly sail *Annette* out past Marstal to the open sea without a pilot ; adding that he had sailed those waters for twenty-seven years but had never been in or out without a pilot. It was a different matter for him, though, as his ship drew five feet and was probably rather cumbersome. *Annette* drew only three feet nine inches and was handy, so that with the assistance of the large-scale chart we had bought at Rudkoping we thought that we could manage without assistance.

As anticipated we had no trouble, except at one point near the harbour of Marstal, where the channel is narrow, and one has to pass within a few yards of the harbour jetty. There we should certainly have come to grief but for the warning shout of somebody ashore who put us on our guard so that we saw the shallow just in time. The channel winds about very much, but, except at the one point where we had the narrow escape from stranding, it is exceedingly well marked, and there is no reason why it should be avoided by a stranger.

Once out in the open sea we encountered a swell which slowed our speed, but the wind freshened and, although it was variable in direction, it came mostly from the northwest and we were able to lie for Kiel. Black squalls of

heavy rain drove from time to time across the sky. The sea
was beautiful, sometimes reflecting the blue of the sky, and
often darkened by the masses of cloud that scurried across
above. *Annette* seemed to rejoice in the freedom of the open
sea and she hurried forward. As the last sight of the coast
astern vanished behind the horizon, the dark mass of
Bulk Head on the German coast could be distinguished,
and the distance to starboard was fringed by a pencil of
land—Jutland.

It was almost dark when Kiel lightship was passed and
we entered the fiord. A German destroyer, long and black,
slipped past ; and a great full-rigged ship, outward bound,
lay across our course on the other tack. It was time to light
our lamps, for barges and steamers were frequently passing.
Frederiksort lighthouse was soon left astern and *Annette II*
fell off a point to the East to make for the little bay of Heikendorf which, from previous experience in *Annette I*, was
familiar to me.

The night was very dark but for the mass of lights at
Holtenau where the great locks of the Kiel Canal marked
a scene of constant activity. The lights of the fiord passenger steamers hurried across from one little pier to another;
buoys were flashing; and *Annette*, with her cabin ports
showing orange and her side lights burning bright, felt
her way into the dark depths of the bay until a sounding
recorded but two fathoms of water, and she swung round as
her anchor fell and the chain roared out.

A pier lay quite close to us but, as I did not remember
having seen it before, the question arose whether it was
Heikendorf or one of the other little bays on the east side
of the fiord. The crew had started to get dinner, but the
immediate prospect of food was dispelled by several steamers

coming for the pier. It seemed that we had anchored in the fairway, and the first steamer was so puzzled with our riding lamp that she planned her course to lie alongside, mistaking us for the pier. A flow of language in German marked the fact that her captain had discovered that we were not a landing-stage but a yacht. The steamer continued her course, passing us by about a couple of feet, and we were subjected to the stolid stare of all her passengers. Two other steamers passed, but neither of them so close and, as we judged they must be the last for the night, the crew carried on with preparations for dinner.

Whilst this was going on I took the opportunity to launch the dinghy and row over towards the pier. Once past this I found three wooden piles, which I knew of old, and both my memory and confidence were refreshed. I then pulled back towards the ship, anxious to be on a larger craft as the steamers when they arrived came so quickly that there was always a chance of being run down. Moreover, there was a more serious point. We were momentarily expecting the arrival of the German Customs launch, and anybody knowing German officialdom will agree that it would have been unwise to have been found rowing back from the shore in a small dinghy when they arrived. One is not allowed to land before the Customs examination has taken place, and it would have been difficult indeed for me to have proved that I had not been ashore.

After dinner we raised anchor and, under the jib, ran past the pier and tied up for the night to one of the posts I had found.

Kiel Fiord is one of those places that is interesting without being attractive. Reference to a chart will show that it is about eight or ten miles long and that a lightship lies at its mouth. The fiord can roughly be divided into two parts : the outer, which is wide and high on the west coast, is cut off from the inner part of the fiord by quite a narrow channel at Frederiksort. The shores of the outer part are comparatively wild and thinly populated; but once inside Frederiksort all the surrounding land is really only a suburb of Kiel but, instead of being connected by train or motor bus, the means of transport is by two lines of fast paddle steamers. The east side is high and woody, and there are numerous little villages where the business men of Kiel have their homes. Heikendorf, where we lay at anchor, was one of these.

The western bank is the commercial quarter and there is practically one continuous line of houses from Kiel, which lies at the end of the fiord, past Holtenau, where the locks are situated, to Frederiksort.

As the Customs had not come to examine us, I assumed that we had either been overlooked or that they did not intend to bother about so small a ship; and we did not trouble to wait for them beyond ten o'clock the morning after our arrival.

We did not care for Kiel. The shops were good, and we accepted the word of a friend that the residential part is well laid out, and the buildings and gardens very fine; but the part we saw was commercial and the people abominably ill-mannered.

The place had altered a good deal since my last visit. In 1923 the times were very bad and many of the people were half starved. The mark had just collapsed and, what with strikes and threats of revolution, the life of the country was at a low ebb. Since then all had changed and the Kiel as seen on this second visit was a very different place. The shops were busy and the prices of provisions were above those in England. The people seemed prosperous and busy. We paid a visit to the English-speaking baker at Heikendorf, who remembered me. He did not agree, however, about the improvements in his country and said times were still bad. Taxes appeared to be his chief complaint, and he told us—though whether it is true I do not know—that the common labourer has to pay seven shillings in the pound of his wages to the Inland Revenue officials.

It took us a day to get in touch with my friend S——, whom I had met in Kiel when there with *Annette I*, but we took an opportunity of going to a bank and doing some shopping. Early on the second morning at Heikendorf an engineer came off from a shipbuilding yard to make a new inlet tube for the motor. He did the work well, and in the afternoon the "smelly monster" broke forth into a happy roar, and *Annette* thundered her way across the fiord to Holtenau where S—— met us. He, in his usual friendly way arranged the whole formality for us, and helped us through the locks into the canal where we lay alongside a string of barges waiting for the convoy that would start next morning. The usual way of arranging to pass through the locks and to be towed through the canal is to engage what S—— called a "shipsmarkler." The shipsmarkler acts as interpreter and quickly does everything that is wanted; but at the same time, unless familiar with the canal charges, the captain is quite in the hands of his broker. For example, the first time that I negotiated the canal I was charged two pounds for towage, when the correct sum should have amounted to but a few shillings. The agents of certain well-known firms are said to be quite straightforward, but

it is not possible for the stranger to distinguish the honest
from the dishonest; and it must be admitted that most
of the shipsmarklers belong to the latter category if judged
by appearances; for a more unhealthy, debauched looking
set of young men it would be hard to imagine.

The total charges for the whole process of being towed
through the canal and out of the locks amounted to fourteen
shillings, on a basis of estimating *Annette's* ship's tonnage
as six tons, for the net tonnage is roughly half the yacht
measurement.

Another yacht was to be in our convoy. She was of
course German, and her skipper was a youthful friend of
the owner's, and as crew he had one paid hand. The
skipper spoke English but, as he was diminutive in stature
and a student by nature, I fancy his authority was greater
when speaking English than when he was actually giving
orders to the hand in his mother tongue. He would say
to us, " Ah, I will tell my sailor so to do! " and then he would
turn to his man and speak in German in a tone that sounded
to us uncommonly like pleading. The hand was a great
contrast to his " master," being small, fat and extremely
self-assertive. His skipper always ended in confiding to
me that " mine sailor thinks that so it is not possible."

It rarely pays to quarrel in foreign waters, so, much as
I disliked the crew of the German yacht, I plied him with
cigars. The fellow liked work. In fact he fussed and pot-
tered with his ropes and our ropes in a way that would
never have occurred to any ordinary mortal.

S—— left us early as he had to get home to his wife
and baby, who were alone in their house at Monkeburg,
near Heikendorf. It had been extraordinarily good of him
to have given so much of his time to helping us at Holtenau.

All the time it had been raining and, as he was very wet, we were sorry he could not stay to dinner. We felt sure his home was safe, as it was guarded by a particularly savage black dog, that although friendly to my wife, refused to allow me into the house when we had visited it during the morning.

During the whole of our voyage we were struck by the small number of dogs we saw. In Denmark it is true that every homestead had its watch dog, and Germany, of course, had many; but the whole of the time we were in Sweden and Gotland we saw but one; and in Latvia dogs were far from numerous.

In the early hours of next morning a lot of shouting brought me on deck. A great steel barge of incalculable length that had been lying astern was preparing to be towed away by the tug, and the ropes from *Annette* and the other yacht had to be shifted. The paid hand from the German yacht was already very excited, and rushed about shouting. He, clad in white woollen pyjamas, looked rather a comic character, and somehow reminded me of an old book of nursery rhymes which contained a picture of a large pink pig attired in scanty but human clothes. A pair of tortoise-shell glasses, behind which lay a thin and yellow face, appeared suddenly from the cabin of the German yacht. It sniffed the air, said " good morning " and, awed by the activity of the sailor, disappeared again with a shiver through the hatch.

I turned in again for a few minutes, and then got out of my bunk to start a Primus going whilst I dressed. Porridge and coffee makes a good start for the day, and I was able to make particularly good coffee as we had for once a bottle of real milk, and at Strynö we had bought some coffee and a pot with which coffee could be made in Danish style. It was a simple contrivance consisting of an enamel coffee pot in which there was a large removable cloth bag for the coffee. It is astonishing how rarely in England one comes across the same arrangement. Danish coffee is ground finer than in our country, and as a rule tastes far better.

At dawn a tug passed emitting a piercing shriek from its syren as a signal that the convoy was to prepare for being towed. I cast off our warps, but passed a single rope round a dolphin, bringing both ends aboard so that it could be cast off at a moment's notice. It was well that I took this precaution for, whilst I was waiting for a second signal from the tug, there was a sudden creak and the rope tautened. I dashed across and cast off; but only just in time, for the convoy had started and the strain must have been immense, as the weight of eight steel barges ahead would have broken ropes and almost torn the dolphin itself away had it been resisted for more than a second.

The sky gradually lightened and the sun rose high. The skipper of the yacht alongside us told me that a report stated that better weather was approaching. It turned out correct and the day was sunny; but we did not care for canal work, and good weather alone was insufficient to make us cheerful.

When two ships tied fore and aft are being towed it is only necessary for one of them to be steered; but I felt no confidence in our neighbouring yachtsman and did not leave the helm for the first two hours. By then, although far from trusting his steering, I thought the ship could safely look after herself with helm lashed whilst I pumped her out; so I left the deck and applied myself to the semi-rotary pump. There was a lot of water aboard and it was a slow business. Suddenly the yacht gave a frightful lurch, which was followed by a shout and a crack like a pistol shot. I dashed on deck and found *Annette* half broadside on to the canal, heeling heavily. I flung myself at the rudder and for a second she hesitated, heeling more, and then like a flash she came back and meekly followed the convoy as if nothing had happened.

The miserable specimen on the next boat had steered right out of his course. The bow rope which was too loose had parted, and the water like a wedge had got between the yachts, whose sterns remained moored together. The German, under her skipper's hand, held her course in safety, but *Annette*, with helm lashed, fell out of line and the more she fell off the greater became the leverage of the water diverting her. The pressure must have been tremendous, but fortunately the stern rope parted, making the report that I had heard and thereby saving the situation.

The danger involved may seem exaggerated to the reader unfamiliar with ships, but it must be remembered that ahead of *Annette* lay eight barges in double line of four each side. The momentum of these hundreds of tons moving at seven knots could have torn *Annette* in pieces with the utmost ease and, had not ropes parted, she must, once broadside on, have been towed broadside on until she capsized.

For a few moments I was too moved to speak, and the humour of the situation did not appeal to me until I saw the sailor disappear below forward, and observed that the German skipper's face had turned green instead of yellow, and a painful smile played round his lips. The escape even of his ship had been narrow, and he was in such a deplorable state of nerves that he kept pushing the helm backwards and forwards, and jerking his head about.

I called my wife, who had finished dressing, and she took charge, although the German owner had the impudence to say she need not trouble, as he would steer for both. Thus we had to take watch by watch throughout the day, whereas the German yacht had an easy time of it, only occasionally steering. My wife caused them some anxiety, I fear, as she steered *Annette* into the middle, pushing the other yacht out of her place; and all their attempts to steer back were of no avail, for their seven tons against our twelve gave them no chance.

At Rensburg the convoy dropped one barge and picked up another. This involved swinging round in a circle and gave me the opportunity of getting the photograph shown.

The tug was extremely powerful, and the journey along the canal was quicker than usual, for we moored near Brunsbüttel at about half-past three. The usual arrangement was to wait there until a different and smaller tug came to tow the convoy through the locks; but the German yacht apparently knew better and, with the encouragement of some cigars, took us in tow and proceeded towards the locks under her powerful motor. Their course could hardly be termed anything but erratic, and I soon much regretted having accepted their assistance. They, with *Annette* following, crossed the locks to the other side of the canal, where they brought up alongside a quay. *Annette's* weight had slowed them up to a considerable extent, and I saw the sailor casting furious glances in our direction; so, when we brought up, and they cast us off, I was extremely suspicious. I was well aware that the skipper wished us well, but I rather doubted the authority he could exert over his hand. They were engaged in a fluent conversation with a harbourmaster and a number of onlookers, and I could hardly get a word out of them when I walked over. We were very much in their hands, for it was doubtful whether our motor would get us to the locks without breaking down and, as we had left the convoy, there was little chance of getting a tow. After a few minutes I got hold of the skipper and put the position in front of him in such a way that he took our tow rope back on board; although complaining that *Annette* was very heavy.

Not trusting their promises in the least, I got the blow lamp going, hoping, in the event of their failing to tow us, that the "smelly monster" would play the game. We waited half an hour and then, observing the skipper walking along the bank in our direction, I found myself confronted by the difficult question of how to disguise the fact that our engine was being prepared for work. I quickly turned the blow lamp low so that it scarcely made a sound, and hurried ashore to meet him. He told us, in rather a dis-illusioned way, that the tug would come for both the yachts after she had taken the convoy into the locks, and that neither of us would be allowed to proceed under our own power.

So it befell that the first should be the last, and after a long wait the tug came for us. It steamed close past us and a man stood amidships with a rope to throw to the German yacht. A tremendous shouting arose at once, and we saw the fat little sailor gesticulating in frantic excitement.

The shouting arose higher and with a simultaneous yell the two ropes were flung, one from each ship and— they met in mid air and subsided into the canal.

The captain of the tug was furious, for the yachts had already given him an extra journey by leaving their proper place at the end of the convoy. The tug swung a large circle and came back; her engines went full speed astern;

and a rope was carefully thrown on the German yacht. The captain rang his engines forward and steamed away, but the yachts?—— The yachts remained behind, for the German had failed to make fast the rope.

We were far from happy for, as the tug steamed away, we thought we should be left behind to wait until the locks opened for the second time; but, when hope had almost gone, we saw the tug swinging round to come back. This time she passed very close and very slowly by the German yacht. Not so much, I fancy, to make it easier, as to enable her captain to let loose a flood of invective. The sailor was obviously abashed and, having made the rope fast, he slunk aft to exchange self-conscious jokes with his skipper. We were cast off in the mouth of the lock and, with a final curse at the German yacht, the tug departed.

We brought up inside the lock with the greatest ease, assisted by two canal porters, but our friends had more trouble and crashed into the wharf ahead. They then were hauled back into a position alongside us.

The skipper came aboard to see my engine, which for some reason he appeared to consider funny. Presently the water filled up the lock, and the time came to get ready. I swung the flywheel twice and put my head on deck where, to my surprise, I saw the Miserable Specimen in a state of incoherence. It appeared that he had been standing talking, when the "smelly monster" suddenly back-fired under his nose with devastating results. He shouted to me anxiously, saying that it was damaging the sides of his yacht. It was true that clouds of smoke were playing round her topsides, and that a series of tremendous reports were taking place within a foot of her white paint; but it did not appear to me to be doing any harm, and I certainly did not intend to stop my motor. Moreover, the noise and smoke had the effect of hurrying them, and the German yacht soon went after bidding us a farewell more gushing than sincere.

The noise had attracted the attention of everybody and, as we started, there followed us along the lock a crowd which included the sluice master and his officials, a vast number of shipsmarklers, four villainous-looking porters and two policemen. The "smelly monster" rose to the occasion, back-firing with incredible fury; bang! tut-tut, bang, bang, bang—BANG!! The crowd started shouting but I, busy with the carburettor, could not hear. Bang, bang, bang! the British yacht was going. . . . Bang, Bang, Bang, Bang!

As soon as we had cleared the locks, we steered round a wooden pier, and brought up in a small space behind, formed by the lock pier and the banked-up shore. The "smelly monster" received my blessings, for it had responded nobly to the call and, although rather self-assertive as regards its tone, it had done its duty.

The German yacht had undoubtedly been a curse to us. When we were in the locks I had asked the skipper to interpret that I wanted to fill up our water tanks; and he had replied there was not time, but that we should be able to do so where we were going. When I went ashore I learnt that the tanks could have been filled up in two minutes in the canal, but where we had tied up it would be necessary for it to be hand-carried from the pilot house. For this work I obtained the help of a somewhat effeminate young man, who was a friend of a ship chandler whom I had engaged to get some provisions. He borrowed a large galvanised-iron tub, which we filled to the brim with water. There was a little hill to be negotiated, and the youth found it most trying, as the water would keep trickling over his shoes and his beautifully creased trousers. He explained to me that he had been a bank clerk, had been dismissed when the staff had been cut down, and then for a time he had been a shipsmarkler to a firm at Brunsbüttel. He seemed unfortunate for he was dismissed there also, and was out of employment waiting for the cash to take him to South America. We made two expeditions from the pilot house to the dinghy with water, at the end of which we were both pretty wet. When the question arose as to remuneration, I explained that I possessed only pound notes, two marks and some cigars. I gave one mark to the woman who had lent the tub, and offered some cigars to the dismissed shipsmarkler for his help. As he said he did not smoke, I presented him with the remaining mark, and promised him another when I should get change from some provisions I was buying. He agreed to this plan at first, but after waiting a little while, he said he would after all rather have cigars. In England one would hardly tip a bank clerk, even if unemployed, but I found in Germany that very few people exist who will not accept money for services rendered.

KIEL FIORD

CHAPTER XII

IN THE NORTH SEA—DOWN THE ELBE—ESTUARY SAILING—
A HEAVY SQUALL—OVERBOARD—ALMOST RUN DOWN—
ALONG THE FRISIAN ISLANDS—BEHIND TEXEL—SAND
BANKS AND CHANNELS—A WRECK—ENTRY TO YMUIDEN
—"FUNNY FELLOWS"—ANOTHER ENGINEER

WE planned our start the next morning very successfully, for *Annette*, under her motor, left the shelter of Brunsbüttel and entered the Elbe just before the flood tide had finished. It was perfect weather, and a nice little breeze from the north filled the sails so that the yacht stemmed the last of the tide, hurried west as it slacked, and then, under the sweep of the freshening wind and the ebb, raced down the river to Cuxhaven. We were very glad to be in the North Sea and, as the glass was high, there was every prospect of being able to sail on for England, with perhaps one night in Ymuiden harbour on the way for rest.

There was a freshness in the air that added zest to the sailing. We were rapidly carried seawards in the creamy brown waters of the Elbe. Both banks of the river were flat, but on the north side they were so low that no land could be seen, and on the south there was but a ribbon of indefinable nature that bounded the water.

After sailing an hour or two we altered course and lay a little more to the south towards Cuxhaven, in order to leave a great sandbank to starboard. The water grew

149

rougher as the stream began to race, and the yacht was carried past Cuxhaven. At that point, owing to a bend in the river, we had to tack, and hardly had time to notice the town, which started in the entrances to its harbours and ended in a line of large houses and hotels facing the sea. On we swept, ever gaining speed as the main rush of the tide increased. Cuxhaven was astern, and to port lay miles of half-covered sands shining yellow in the sun. To starboard a line of buoys bent their pointed cones to seaward and a trail of foam and wavelets marked the tide as it raced past.

We were getting into more exposed waters and the sea, worried between wind and tide, rose in a fury of little waves. Great steamers passed constantly, and about us lay the endless variety of other shipping to be met with in the estuaries of busy ports. Through a pass over the sands to the south a little yacht hurried, and a glance through the binoculars confirmed the idea that she was the German with whom we had been towed through the Canal. They were unquestionably making for shelter, and an hour or so would see them safely back at Cuxhaven.

On sailed *Annette* and, when Elbe III lightship was abeam, it was blowing hard from the north-west and a big sea was running. About three times we had to tack across the river and, but for the tide racing out, it would have taken a very long time. Near Elbe II lightship we passed a fleet of fishing boats and the skipper of an incoming trawler, seeing the Red Ensign and that we were outward bound, saluted us with his syren and waved his arm.

How long would the tide last? By then it was due to turn and, once against us, we should be bottled in the river for six hours unless we could get over the corner of the Scharhörn sands where we should get a fair wind west. In spite of the splendid system of buoyage, navigation was not so easy as might be imagined. Land of course was out of sight, and we were tacking out of an estuary bounded on each side by shoals, and the sea was so rough that it was far from easy to see even the tall red spar buoys, unless a tack happened to bring the yacht in fairly close proximity to one.

The Thames has a bad name, but the entrance to the Elbe is comparable to the Thames mouth turned round to face the prevailing winds. A more exposed position than the entrance to the rivers Elbe, Jade and Weser would be difficult to imagine.

Fortune favoured us and, in spite of calculations, we managed to beat as far out as Elbe I lightship before the tide turned. From there we could lay west, with but slight alteration of course, for two or three days. The low line of the Frisian Islands would lie to the south with their treacherous outlying sands, but our course would take us past a series of lightships about ten miles out at sea, and it was not likely that we should see land, even in the distance.

The crew turned in and I took the first watch. Once in the open sea, free from the estuary tide, the water was not so rough although, of course, a heavy swell was running. Westward sailed the ship, on and on, and the sun fell lower and lower. Occasionally a buoy was passed, marking our progress, which was slow owing to the contrary tide. When night fell the Roter Sand and Wangeroog flashed to port, and the sky to the north-east was from time to time pierced by white rays from Heligoland.

The crew took a watch and I took a sleep. The Weser lightship was passed, but a certain amount of uncertainty existed with regard to its light as, when I turned in, it had not been in sight, and during the subsequent watch of the crew nothing was passed but a weak fixed light—not what was indicated on the chart as the Weser. However, when my turn to take the helm came again, both watch and log showed that the lightship must be well astern.

The weather looked threatening and rather shook our confidence in the wisdom of trusting to the barometer, which was high and steady. The sky to the north was gradually becoming overcast by a mass of black cloud. Thunder muttered in the distance and the wind freshened. It continued to freshen, and the heavy bank of cloud approached steadily, blotting out the stars. The waves began to break and the yacht heeled over and plunged forward into the night through the foaming water. I dropped the mizzen and prepared for trouble.

The squall struck us.

The wind screamed and a flash of lightning lit the breaking waves from horizon to horizon.

Then came the rain in one huge burst. The sea hissed with its violence; hail came roaring on the deck and drove into my face; and every light of ship and lighthouse disappeared behind the veil of utter darkness.

It had passed, and the yacht lay becalmed, rolling in a heavy swell with her decks covered with hail stones. She rolled and pitched and rolled again. The booms crashed madly to and fro; the sails shook; and somewhere in the distant cabin some loose bottles clinked in empty misery.

The side lights had been extinguished and a steamer was

bearing down at us. The crew slipped to the helm, whilst I went forward to relight the lamps. I put the starboard light in its place and, with the port lamp in my hand, crept forward again on the reeling deck, reached the shrouds and began screwing it in place. A sudden lurch, fiercer than the rest, threw me off my balance and in a second cold water rushed up to meet me. One arm was crooked round a shroud and, as I fell, I managed to grasp it in my hand. For a moment I lay suspended half in the sea, and then with one effort, as the ship lurched in the other direction, I was aboard again.

The lamp was out and the red and green lights of the steamer lay straight on the port bow, and the yacht rolled helpless in the waves. I rushed aft and had almost gained the companion when something happened, and I found myself lying on the weather deck. The boom had struck me on the forehead. The crew shouted something and pushed an electric torch into my hands. In a moment I was by the lee mizzen shrouds and, with my arms embracing these, I flashed the torch through the red glass of the lamp.

The steamer came on, and the yacht rolled lifeless in the deep. The side light was smoky and the feeble rays of the cheap hand torch had not the strength to pierce the sooted glass. As a last resort I flashed the torch free at the oncoming ship, and shouted at the crew to wave the riding lamp that lay hidden in the steering well; but the moment it was raised I could see that it was too dirty to avail much, and the torch that I held was but a minute speck in the darkness.

On came the ship, now so close that her side lights looked far apart and high up.

On she came, and we prepared for the impact—two life-buoys lay handy, lightly tied to the mizzen shrouds.

All was noise, but above all could be heard a sound of thrashing water, and the port lamp of the steamer disappeared whilst a green light glimmered above us, and a great black hull lay across our bow.

At the last moment we had been seen, the ship had altered course and backed her engines. Probably it was the light of the cabin lamp shining through the portholes that had saved us.

The ship passed on, and *Annette* presently moved west again, fanned forward by a steadily increasing breeze.

To describe a passage of this nature takes but a few lines of a book, except where some exciting incident breaks the monotony. It is only the exceptional circumstances that call for comment; but the reader will understand that all the steady sailing, the changes of watch, and the anxieties must lie between the lines. Thus *Annette* sailed west all that night and all next day, with nothing but the passing of the Norderney and Borkum lightships to break the monotony; yet all the time the resources of skipper and crew were constantly tried.

Shortly after the narrow escape from being run down, a nice wind came up and, with the exception of one or two passing squalls, it continued fresh from the north and the yacht steadily forged ahead.

On the following afternoon the Dutch island of Ameland appeared on the port bow and, when evening fell, a light from its summit, and lights from one or two other islands made our exact position certain. By nightfall we were off the gat between the islands of Terschelling and Vlieland; the lightship lay a few miles further to seaward. Unfortunately the wind had backed more to the west, heading us off, and it was not long before it fell off, leaving *Annette* practically becalmed. The motor was run for a few hours until a scorching smell and a little wisp of steam showed that the stern bearing had got overheated. The tide was against us, so, when dawn broke, we found ourselves in almost the same place as we had been the previous evening. But for the fact that we sailed the whole length of German North Sea coast, and scored some hundred and fifty sea miles, we should have been sorely disappointed; particularly as when the wind did pick up again at 5 a.m. it came from the west; absolutely contrary to our course.

By then we had been sailing continually for forty-eight hours, and were so far from fresh that the prospect of another twenty-four hours of slowly beating to windward was agreed by skipper and crew to be most unpleasant. Accordingly *Annette's* bow paid off, swung in a circle until, after a gybe, she headed south for the Terschelling See gat, that lay between the islands. The channel was clearly marked and the crew piloted our ship safely on through the brown-coloured sea. We were quite soon in sheltered water under Vlieland, for the wind was very fresh and drove *Annette* over the strong ebb tide. The channel took us close to the low island whose clean sandy shores, on which the ebb left pools of water, were the refuge of numberless wild fowl. The lighthouse on a sand dune came abeam, and *Annette* altered course a trifle to clear a line of dancing white foam, which revealed the presence of a submerged sand bank.

There are two " gats " through the outlying shoals between the islands; and, once inside these, navigation is complicated by the junction of some other channels; and the crew had to strain her eyes to see that a short cut from one channel to another was not taken inadvertently. It was almost low tide and, behind Vlieland, we saw a creek leading through the sand banks to a village. We were skirting another great sand bank; and, about a mile away, the hull of a fishing boat at anchor in some channel looked as though it were high and dry on the sands. The scenery was, in its forlorn way, very beautiful, for the sun lit up the yellow banks, and shone through the shallow water, lighting it in pale shades of green and brown. Off the shoals, now bare, little trickles of water came pouring down in miniature cascades to join the silent swift ebb tide.

Suddenly we became aware of a dark cloud to starboard stretching from sea to sky and approaching fast. It appeared to be revolving. The air thickened and a whirling mass of cloud and rain rushed past at furious speed, blotting out the sun, and obscuring sea, sky and land in one indistinct yellow blur. The wind freshened for a moment but the waterspout passed ahead, leaving us untouched.

We had calculated on having the stream with us, but our plans were certainly at fault, for a hot tide ran against us for the greater part of the day. Presently we came to a very big division where two channels joined, and we took the turn along the more westerly, bringing the wind ahead. Try as we might we could make no way against the ebb until we crossed over the channel and started tacking over the shallow water just outside of the fairway. In this way we sailed on for a couple of hours, slowly creeping over the tide. We only touched the bottom once, and then got off again with the greatest ease by lifting the centre board. No other ship came our way, other than a couple of Dutch pilot boats which, under powerful motors, soon passed us.

After lunch we invoked the aid of the "smelly monster" for an hour, and it helped us on well until the stern bearing became so hot that the engine had to be stopped. All the afternoon and evening we tacked on in a steadily lightening breeze along a narrow, winding little channel. On the ship went, coaxed with the greatest care, for we wanted to negotiate a difficult bend before darkness fell as, once round that, two leading lights would enable us to navigate the channel. Night crept on slowly, unnoticed, and buoys became more and more difficult to see, but, just as the last hint of light had vanished, *Annette* reached the first lighted buoy. Far away a little red speck flashed out to show the course, but with night the last flicker of wind fell away. We let the yacht be swept along the channel by the tide, which was then fair; but after a short time we had to anchor to avoid being set on to a sand bank.

Annette lay to her anchor, the tide swept past, and but for the occasional call of a sea bird, all was quiet. The utter solitude was very wonderful. Our little world lay in a narrow channel of water surrounded by miles and miles of half-covered sand banks and mussel beds. I hoisted a riding lamp forward, and then went below for a quick meal, before turning in, when I fell asleep the moment my head touched the pillow.

Next morning there was more breeze and the yacht sailed at good speed, assisted by the ebb tide. The little channel was soon left behind and *Annette* swept down the great Texel Stroom along the sandy southern shores of Texel Island. It was a grand morning and was in itself a compensation for any hardships that had been our lot.

The sea was very smooth as the wind was light, and the island made a breakwater to the outside swell. We brought the gramophone on deck and played our full programme of records. Why a gramophone should be the object of scorn I cannot imagine. It is true that it gives but a scratchy rendering of music and the tone is shallow; but, after all, there is no necessity to notice its shortcomings. The ear need not hear the scratchings and what is wanting in tone may be made up for by imagination. Moreover, the musical man is often romantic, which in itself indicates the power of blindness.

This part of the cruise had an additional interest to me, as on my previous voyage I had sailed in the Zuider Zee and among the islands east of Schiermonnikoog. Thus the present cruise completed my familiarity with the whole chain of islands facing the North Sea.

Towards midday we came to the gat leading to the North Sea past Helder. Helder is the naval port of Holland, and we passed a warship and a submarine as we sailed by the town. It had taken about six hours to gain the North Sea, so that we had but the afternoon and evening left in which to make port before night. The tide after lunch was against us, but a fresher breeze enabled the yacht to stem it easily, and the line of sand dunes, marking the coast of Holland, rapidly slipped past as we sailed south. Occasionally the land was protected by dykes instead of sand hills, but, with those exceptions, the monotony was only relieved once where the massive wreck of some warship lay half-capsized along the shore. It was dusk when we passed, and night fell long before we were in reach of harbour. Fortunately, Ymuiden, the next port, was very well lighted, and we had no difficulty in locating and entering it. A pilot steamer in the offing came close to us and made signals which we could not understand; so we sailed on for the red and green lights that marked the end of the piers. Before midnight we brought up in the outer harbour, just out of the fairway. On each side of our anchorage ran two curved moles; close to us a tall white lighthouse flashed an electric blaze into the sky, and further up the harbour the air glowed with the reflected glare from the busy locks that open into the North Sea Canal leading to Amsterdam.

The paragraphs above again illustrate very well that a few words will convey the doings of a considerable time. They contain the actions of a day from dawn to midnight. At the end of that time we were tired, and admitting the reader may also have been tired with the paragraphs, his weariness cannot possibly approach that of the navigators who carried out the contents in fact.

After three days without touching port provisions were running low, so *Annette* next day was sailed into the inner harbour and, with the assistance of several willing onlookers, tied up alongside a stage.

I am sure not even a townsman of Ymuiden could take much pride in his birthplace. It is very little more than a village and owes its existence to the construction of the canal to Amsterdam. All of the buildings are quite modern and, although no doubt very sanitary, would, I fear, utterly fail to inspire even the most versatile of poets. We visited the post office for letters, and then had a lunch at a third-rate restaurant. Whilst sitting there waiting for the meal to be served our attention was aroused by strains of music in the street. A travelling band was marching past, and the antics of the window cleaners outside were very amusing

—much more so than the band. One of these was a large fellow of very Dutch appearance, not unlike the Dutchmen depicted on china wearing trousers with sterns a size too large for them. He and his " mate " were carrying a ladder between them and at once started dancing to the music with the ladder swinging a rhythm very dangerous to passers by.

After we had recovered from this spectacle we set out provisioning and then went straight back to the ship and got under way. We decided we wanted at any price to get back to England, and accordingly set a course straight across the North Sea for Lowestoft.

After sailing for some hours, and having left the powerful light of Ymuiden below the horizon, a heavy squall struck us. Thinking that it was the beginning of a gale, we ran back to harbour in company with a fleet of Urk fishing boats.*

We brought up and tied to a large dolphin in a basin on the east side of the harbour at some early hour next morning. It was most unfortunate that we should have tired ourselves with an unsuccessful attempt at crossing the North Sea, for, as it turned out the wind moderated and, if we had been fresh, it would have been perfectly practicable to have started in the daytime. As it was, we slept on until midday when, disturbed by the continual shouting of some men loading gravel on barges near by, we finally decided to get up. *Annette* was sailed across the harbour and tied up in her old berth at the staging in order

---

* This fleet has its fishing grounds in the North Sea, but the home port is at Urk, a little island in the Zuider Zee. The fishing boats are typically Dutch and, but for the recent introduction of auxiliary motors, are just as they were a hundred years ago.

to be near the shops. We lunched at a different hotel, which proved to be even worse than that we had visited the day before.

In the afternoon we entertained some newly found acquaintances to tea. Two of these were old seafaring men who had helped us moor up *Annette*, and had given us advice about one or two other little matters. They were nice simple souls, and a great contrast to a young man who had walked over with me to the locks to interpret the weather report that was posted on a notice board there. He hastened to explain that he had been a cavalry officer in the Dutch regular army; and there was little in his conversation that failed to impress us with his importance. His English was so perfect that only one word existed that he did not know and that was " snob." He managed to whisper that our other guests were " funny fellows," and they, who I am sure had no pretensions or aspirations to blue blood, soon departed, no doubt feeling unfit to be seated at the same table as the self-designated aristocrat.

News of a British yacht in a small harbour soon travels, so I was not surprised when I was found out by the man who had acted for me as pilot in the Zuider Zee in 1923. We had not left on the best of terms, but time had healed any feelings of hostility and we greeted each other as long-lost friends. He was quite a good fellow really, and at once set to work to see what he could do for us. He was much impressed with my new ship and looked over her with the greatest admiration, describing her as " a Dutch ship with a leeboard in her middle." My opinion of the "smelly monster" evidently pained him, and he suggested that he should fetch a young engineer who was very clever with paraffin engines. He went, and, after an absence of about half an hour returned with his friend, who cleared the inlet to the cylinder and claimed, like all the other engineers, to have analysed the illness of the "smelly monster." He departed after a few minutes with four guilders in his pocket but I, knowing perfectly well that the engine would break down again before it had run many miles, sat down to meditate on the cause of the trouble. Six engineers had failed to put the matter right, but as the trouble was invariably due to dirt in the injector the cause could not be very far to seek. I emptied out the fuel tank and brought it on deck. As I had anticipated, I found there quite a quantity of rust and dirt. Having thoroughly cleaned this out the trouble was solved and I patted the "smelly monster" on its reeking cylinder head, admitting that its failures were entirely due to the stupidity of its master.

The pilot and I discussed the best means of getting to England. As it was so late in the year, he thought the best plan was to pass through the canals under auxiliary power, and along the Dutch waterways behind the islands to Flushing. The crew and I, however, had no liking for ditch crawling; and decided that, if it was in any way possible, we should sail south or west across the North Sea on the morrow. The weather report was not very encouraging—" Winds, south to south-west, with possibility of a storm "; but the tables showed that the wind was south-east in places, and there was a possibility of a fair wind. The pilot agreed that it would certainly be quicker to cross straight to England, so we shook hands and bade farewell.

About midnight we were disturbed by a creaking and a wash of water on the ship's side. I went on deck and found that a fierce rush of water was pressing *Annette* against the staging, where her inefficient fenders entirely failed to prevent the rubbing strake from being severely crushed. It was low tide and the locks were opened in order to lower the height of water inside the canal. After a couple of hours it ceased, but it is worthy of mention, as other foreign yachtsmen might get in trouble if unprepared for the possibility of meeting a strong current inside the harbour.

DEEP SEA CRUISING

CHAPTER XIII

THE PASSAGE PERILOUS——FOR ENGLAND BOUND——LIGHT WIND
——DAWN AND A FALLING GLASS——MID-NORTH SEA——
HARD WIND——SUNSET——THE THUNDER OF THE STORM——
A GRAND SCENE——PASSING HOURS——LOST AT SEA——THE
RED EYES OF THE GALLOPER——A FIERCE RUN FOR HARBOUR
——A WILD EXPANSE OF WHITE-CAPPED OCEAN——KENTISH
KNOCK——HARBOUR——THE VOYAGE ENDED

AT dawn, September 18th, *Annette* with mainsail and jib set to a light southerly breeze, and with motor throbbing with successful effort, slowly made her way out of Ymuiden. The lighthouse, whose flashing beam was still visible in the weak light of early morning, was passed, and the yacht steadily threaded her course between the double lines of little harbour buoys, and out between the mole heads to the open sea, where she curtseyed to the freedom of the waves.

Her course lay a little south of west, and if distance could have been pierced by some powerful eye, the English coast of Suffolk could have been seen some hundred and few odd miles in the direction to which the bows of the ship were pointing. The hands of the clock in the cabin marked the passing hours, and knot after knot of grey moving waves were forced apart, as the vessel ploughed her wilful way seaward. The Dutch coast from a yellow sandy ribbon fell to but a mark of grey pencilled against the vague horizon, and then slowly lessened until the moment arrived when keen eyes strained hard saw it no more.

The wind freshened and *Annette* hurried forward under the greater force, and the occasional whip of spray flashed from her bows to fall with a hiss on the deck and tumble out along the lee scuppers and back to the sea. After a few hours a shift of wind enabled the course to be altered, and, with the limitless expanse of grey waves in every direction, the yacht steered south.

Morning passed; the sun came out and having reached its highest limit began to fall in its curved path to the west; and when it reddened with its last strength the yacht might have been seen passing a few miles outside the Maas lightship. For the crew of two there had been little rest; for watch by watch the ship had to be steered, and the one who was off duty at the helm, had time occupied in cooking, in washing up, or in calculating tides and courses, or in adjusting sails, tightening halyards, cleaning lamps and in carrying out other innumerable duties.

The evening meal was eaten, the crockery packed away and night had fallen. Astern the flashes from the Maas lightship and the Hook of Holland pierced the darkness; abeam a series of winking lights indicated the islands from which long shoals extended miles to sea; and on the port bow a glow in the sky, reflected at intervals, betokened the presence of the Schouwen lightship. The wind was light and though, throughout the long hours, the yacht steadily forged ahead, yet a powerful tide held her back so that the whole night's sail failed to bring the Schouwen abeam.

The crew had taken the cold watch at dawn and, when daylight came, no land, no ship could be discerned to break the horizon in any direction. Lightness of wind and slightness of sea had failed to make the night watches easy, for the helmsman had to keep open a vigilant eye, as *Annette* had passed through a fleet of fishing boats, and several steamers had crossed her course. Two hurricane lights, one green and one red, had been purchased at Ymuiden to supplement the inefficient side lights, and these, kept lighted and hidden in the steering well, had to be shown as required when a ship passed close.

In cruising the most depressing time is the first dawn at sea. The romance of the night sailing has passed; the fatigue through the constant buffeting of the ship, and the weariness owing to lack of sleep combines with cold wetness of early morning to make the position of helmsman anything but enviable. Perhaps what adds more than anything to the physical discomfort of the hour, is the fact that little food has been eaten in the preceding eight hours. In our case there was another difficulty in long sea passages, in the fact that neither the crew nor myself were sufficiently good sailors to be able to do much cooking or washing up without grave danger of succumbing to the popular malady of the sea. Thus, whatever was eaten must of necessity have been very simple: bread and butter, eggs and tinned provisions. The difficulty of what to drink was even more serious, for when the waves were in any way rough we could only obtain water mixed with rust and dirt from the tank—which was built into the yacht, so that it could not be cleaned without the greatest difficulty. We filtered this water through a handkerchief, but even then it was far from palatable and only fit for cooking. Tea on a ship is always very unsatisfactory unless fresh milk is available; and the same drawback applies to coffee. The drinks that we found suitable were but two: beer and Horlick's Malted Milk. Unfortunately, when very rough and we were very tired we did not fancy beer, and not feeling well enough to boil and mix Horlick's, we drank nothing at all.

To return to the subject of dawn off the Dutch coast. It was cold and damp as is usual, but *Annette* was sailing well on her course to Dover and the cheerful prospect of being soon at England made us forget our less happy physical condition. The glass was falling and the wind freshening, so *Annette* sailed fast towards the south. The tide was fair and we hoped to see the North Hinder lightship in the early afternoon. The morning passed and in every direction lay a waste of sea. We were off the mouths of the Schelde and a trail of submerged sands bounded the Dutch coast, far out of sight to port. A sailing ship passed across our course, bound probably for Flushing. The glass was steadily falling tenth by tenth, and the wind was fresh in the extreme. The question of running into Flushing or Ostende passed across my mind but was quickly dismissed, for all those coasts are hemmed in by treacherous shoals; and, moreover, we were not sure of our position. When sailing slowly in seas where the tides run fast it is extremely difficult to calculate one's exact position and, before closing with a dangerous coast, it is imperative to have a reasonably reliable idea of the ship's place. Fairways and shoals may look clearly marked on a chart but, when it comes to practical experience, it is only too easy to fail to see a buoy, to mistake one for another, or to make insufficient or over-sufficient allowance for tide and leeway.

During the previous night we had been almost drifting at the mercy of currents and, whilst admitting that I had a fairly accurate idea of our position, yet it did not seem sufficient reason to warrant me closing with the shores of Holland or Belgium.

On we sailed and at about 2 p.m. I felt very anxious, for we had failed to pick up the North Hinder lightship. When hope had almost gone a spidery red form could be vaguely discerned ahead and in less than an hour we passed close to the lightship. My calculation had been exact as regards course, but our speed had been over-estimated. The whole crew of the lightship turned out to see us, but I had no time even to wave a reply to their signal; for a squall had struck us and I was busy reefing the mainsail.

By then it was blowing half a gale and the glass had fallen six tenths since morning. The Sandettié lightship lay about thirty miles to the south and from the Sandettié to Dover it was but a matter of another twenty; so cost what it might we determined to sail on for England. *Annette* foamed forward on her way.

The reader, if he be acquainted with sailing, will probably wonder why I had not reefed the yacht close in view of the threatening conditions. The question will occur to him because he is unfamiliar with *Annette*. *Annette II*, of twelve tons and immense stability, carried less canvas than *Annette I*, my former little six-tonner. Her sails were also more evenly distributed over her length than is the case with most ships. To prepare for heavy weather I carried a small jib, a reefed mainsail and the mizzen. The reefed mainsail was borne instead of a trysail because it might be necessary to beat to windward, and a trysail is no use for sailing by the wind. The mizzen was carried in case it should be necessary to heave-to.

On sailed *Annette*, and the wind freshened until she was thrashing her way through rough water; but the sea was not very high, for the wind being a trifle east of south came off the distant shore of Belgium. Time passed and the glass continued to fall. It had dropped eight tenths since morning.

Half-way to Sandettié it happened; but what happened I cannot exactly describe, for I was too stunned by its violence to observe much.

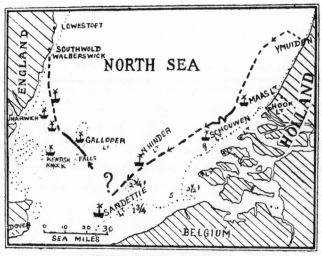

A STORM IN THE NORTH SEA

The sun had been low and fiercely yellow, and a great bank of purple cloud gradually crawled across the sky from horizon to horizon. The sun was hidden, but a wan light lit up the white-capped sea. Suddenly the waves were obscured in whiteness and there was a sizzling noise. The ship reeled, the rigging shrieked and every spar, every rope, tautened under the fury of the first stroke of the gale. Steering was useless, for the ship lay first up into the wind, and then off the wind, lifeless, and the waves leapt short, steep and breaking. The heavy oak hatch to the companion was down, the dinghy on the foredeck was lashed down by four ropes. All was safe. A wave leapt aboard, broke and came running over the cabin top and off to leeward. Out ran the mainsheet, for the lee rail was under. That eased her, and I pulled the jib to weather. *Annette* lay hove-to with mizzen hard sheeted. I lashed the helm and sàt in the steering well. What really took place I do not know. I think the rain lasted for some time. I believe there was thunder and lightning, but it was the force of the wind that was so stunning. I ought to have lowered the mainsail, but I did not do so.

Seizing an opportunity between the waves I opened the hatch and slipped into the warm interior of the cabin.

With the gale the wind had shifted to the south-west, at once dispelling all hope of gaining the safety of Dover. Hove-to on the port tack we were slowly drifting out to mid-North Sea, but the danger really lay in the wind shifting to west or north-west, for then the Belgian coast would be less than twenty miles under our lee.

I was of course very wet, for no oilskins could resist the sweep of the downpour. I lay on my bunk ; it was the only thing to do, and even that was difficult owing to the violent motion of the yacht.

The crew had been busy with the lamps : white, green and red, which were all jammed between the table and a bunk, where they were ready for use. She had also prepared malted milk, and this, together with some dry biscuits, formed our evening meal. What it meant to filter water, and boil it, and to mix the powdered milk, in the close atmosphere of the reeling cabin the reader may hardly be capable of understanding. When fit and well, a few hours on deck in heavy weather is most exhilarating, but when tired, and confined to a cabin in a gale on a pitch black night the matter is very different; and how the crew managed even the moderate amount of cooking she performed without being sick seemed to me miraculous.

At night the lights of steamers passed near, and occasionally the crew or myself went on deck to show lights. The scene was grand in the extreme. Black waves with roaring, white tops came rushing on top of the hard-pressed ship. Up lifted her bow straight to meet one, down it fell on the sloping mass of water into the hollow, and then up again it would shoot just in time to climb some hissing monster. Sometimes the top of one would flop aboard and fall with a thud on the top of the cabin, to stream aft over the closed companion. There was tremendous noise; probably wind amongst the spars and rigging; but above all raged a continual " thrumming." I believe the sea steadily increased, for the motion became worse and worse. Two of the lamps got smashed, but it did not matter, as they flickered so much when exposed to the wind that they would not have been of much use; moreover, we were too tired to go on deck and were quite game to take the chance of perhaps one in ten thousand of being run down.

The position was romantic in the extreme: hove-to in the night of an equinoctial gale, surrounded at a distance of about twenty miles, except to the north, by a broken circle of shoals. We were absolutely in the hands of chance. In actual fact, however, this coloured point of view did not occur to either of us until long after we were safely in port. At the time we were profoundly miserable. We just lay on our bunks, barely conscious, yet not sleeping. The position was not so imminently dangerous so long as the wind did not shift to the west; but it was utterly wretched, and the endless hammering and shaking were tiring, not to speak of the continual effort required to prevent being thrown off the bunks.

The chances were that we should have to let ourselves be picked up by some passing steamer.

The night went by steadily, but neither slowly nor quickly: it just went by.

Through the portholes the sky became a little lighter, and the crew suggested that, as it was my turn, I should go on deck to see if any lights were in sight, for we had but a vague idea where we were drifting; as when the storm had started we had been out of sight of any lightship. I remained where I was for some minutes, before summoning energy to slip on deck. It was bitterly cold and a big sea was running, but the force of the wind was not so great as it had been. To my surprise, reflected in the sky to the west I saw the frequent glare of several distant flashing lights. We had either drifted towards the Thames mouth, or had we in some way been driven close to the Belgian coast? The latter possibility was not very probable, but if such was the case *Annette* was already in danger.

Suddenly away on the starboard quarter a red flash glowed, and went. It came again, and then followed a long wait before it reappeared.

Two minutes before the sight of this lightship, we were lost at sea in a gale; but in those hundred odd seconds the situation was utterly changed, for, instead of being lost, the ship's position was known. Little as I knew the Thames mouth I could not be misled by the two red flashes. On the face of the whole chart they could mean but one thing— the Galloper lightship.

The wind, which had shifted from time to time during the night, was south-south-west in the early hours of the

morning. The helm was unlashed, the jib sheeted to leeward and the yacht began to sail fast to the west. As she
gathered way and flung herself forwards, the great seas
leapt at her bows and spray was hurled in massive sheets
by the screaming wind. With a roar a big sea flung itself
aboard, struck the dinghy, and pattered over the cabin.
A few minutes later another reared up and came crashing
over the ship, breaking in solid mass over the companion
cover, and a loose corner of its fury lashed by the wind
struck me a heavy blow across my chest. All night we
had lain in our bunks damp to the skin and, now in the
bitter cold before dawn, the ice-cold water drove through
our oilskins.

On went the ship in the wild scene. Time after time
waves swept her from stem to stern, and rushed harmlessly
off her decks to leeward. The danger was past, but the
experience was yet far from over. Hope, kindled by a certain
knowledge of our position, together with the sting of spray
and the whip of the wind, made it possible to carry on and
almost enjoy the trial.

The main trouble was that we were utterly worn out
during the night with the effort of keeping ourselves from
rolling off our bunks, but hunger was another serious want,
for, under such conditions, cooking was almost impossible.
A little warmth was suffused by sips of whisky, Riga
balsam, and the edge of hunger relieved by macaroons
purchased at Ymuiden. The latter were soon wet, as a
wave arrived at the exact moment the tin was opened.

The Galloper light came abeam and the yacht left it
about three miles to starboard. The sea was tremendous
and very confused; which was due to the fact that we were
passing over comparatively shallow water.

The crew sat beside me trying to make out the distant flashing glows in the sky. I do not mention her behaviour during this fight for harbour, as whatever hardships I suffered were felt by her to a much greater extent, as she was more unused to such extreme physical strain, and in any case, she was not very strong. Moreover, I, who was responsible for bringing the crew into the torment of a gale, was utterly and profoundly miserable; yet she, more exhausted and more nervous of the two, kept cheerful when things were at their worst, and took her full share in any work that she could do.

An hour passed, but the lights themselves still remained out of sight, and presently the electric reflections could no longer be distinguished from the lightening sky.

I had never sailed before on the east coast, and my North Sea chart which covered the Thames mouth was of too small scale to be of any use. The other chart was a Blue Back, also of small scale, and several years old. We were not in fit condition to carry out any intricate navigation, the sea was heavy and the chances of seeing any of the light-ships and finding the buoys leading to Harwich were poor. If we could but have got within sight of the " Sunk " in darkness all might have been well, but in the faint flashes in the distance we could not distinguish the Sunk, Long Sand or even Kentish Knock lightship.

The wind, moreover, threatened to veer more to the west, so, rather than attempt the tricky entrance to Harwich without a proper chart, we eased the sheets and *Annette* fled northwards for Lowestoft.

In the furious sea and before the fierce wind the yacht needed every ounce of strength to keep her on her course. It was hard and exhausting work and, in the misery of the cold, the time seemed hardly to pass. The crew tried to take a watch, but the effort was beyond her physical strength, and she could not hold *Annette* straight. Hours and hours seemed to have gone by and the time came when land should have been in sight. One or two steamers passed and the sea seemed to be moderating, but nothing, nothing but waves lay in every direction.

On sailed the ship, on and on and on; but no land came in sight and the misery of uncertainty began to creep into our minds.

Suddenly the crew saw something on the port bow; and, in spite of my not being able to see anything but the foam-broken mass of sea, I knew the end of our difficulties was in sight. The crew went below and got a Primus going to heat the cabin. The sea was steadily moderating, and presently the crew reappeared on deck with a tin of cold baked beans, which between us we devoured. She then took a watch, and I went below into the warmth of the cabin, peeled off my oilskins and slowly changed into dry clothes.

This took an hour and when next I went on deck, with dry clothes on my exterior and whisky in my interior, I felt a different man, but my wife, who was also wet through, would not change. A low coast was abeam, and short brown waves replaced the confused mass of breaking sea.

A black buoy was passed, the sun appeared, but the minutes still seemed like hours. At last we saw a town on the port bow and after some consideration came to the conclusion that it was Southwold. It came nearer and, through the glasses, we distinguished two long low wooden piers. Reference to the *Cruising Association Handbook* gave a few notes on the harbour which were far from encouraging, but on nearer approach we realised that we had a leading wind up the reach between the piers. The yacht sailed more inshore, the entrance came near and we could see the waves breaking on either side. We calculated it was two hours after high water, but the sea did not look shallow in front of the harbour, and, as Lowestoft lay twelve miles away, we determined to try to gain port at once, and sailed on straight for the piers. I took two soundings with the lead; and a moment later *Annette* foamed up the entrance and her anchor dropped in the calm water of the harbour.

The voyage was at an end.

UNPREJUDICED OPINIONS OF THE GALE

NEWSPAPER REPORTS

Sunday Times, September 20*th.*

WEEK-END GALE

LITTLE DAMAGE TO MILITARY CAMPS

HEAVY RAIN GENERAL

(By our Weather Correspondent.)

The week-end gave rise to very wet and rough weather over practically all parts of England and Wales. This change was brought about by the development of a new disturbance off the north coast of Spain early on Saturday morning. Warm air, drawn from the region of the Azores, caused a rapid development of this system, and very soon pressure at its centre was lower than for the parent system, which had persisted near Iceland during the whole of the week. This new depression travelled north-eastwards across England at a rate of approximately 50 m.p.h., and gave rise to gales along most parts of the English Channel and high winds inland, *which, in gusts, exceeded gale force.*

Daily Mail, September 21st.

GALES AND STORMS

WORST WEEK-END OF THE YEAR

AEROPLANE IN A SNOWSTORM

Violent gales and fierce rainstorms swept over many parts of Great Britain during the week-end and left much havoc in their trail.

Many vessels were in distress around the coasts, cross-Channel air expresses received severe buffeting, exciting flood rescue scenes occurred at Birmingham, and hundreds of trees and hoardings were blown down in various parts of the country. Wireless aerials were wrecked, motoring at Brooklands was stopped, and football matches were interfered with. Altogether it was the worst week-end of the year.

At Dungeness, Kent, a 40-miles-an-hour wind raged from 9 o'clock on Saturday evening till 5 o'clock yesterday morning. At Calshot, Hants, and *Spurn Head, Yorkshire,* the gale reached a speed of about *50 miles an hour.*

LINER'S DRIFT

The Royal Mail Steam Packet Company's liner Orbita (9,392 tons net), bound from Southampton to New York, ran aground on the shingle bank in the Needles Channel at the western end of the Isle of Wight at 4.30 on Saturday. The Yarmouth lifeboat and tugs put out to her assistance, but she refloated under her own steam at 8 o'clock and was able to proceed on her way undamaged.

The Orbita had just dropped the pilot who had brought her down the Solent, when in the heavy gale and strong tide she drifted on to the dangerous bank. At one time she had a heavy list, but she gradually righted herself.

A FRIEND FOUND

CHAPTER XIV

CLEANING UP—THE "BELL" OF WALBERSWICK—RETROSPECT

THE harbour is a mile from the town of South-wold itself, and is situate on a little river by a small village named Walberswick. We had at first anchored just within the piers, but, after a short wait, the harbour-master's man boarded us, and helped *Annette* to a better place past the ferry, where she could lie alongside a wooden staging. Everything below in the cabin was soaked through, and the water in the bilges was up to the floor boards, but never in our lives had we felt more happy. We were not only in port, but in England; although miles from the home port of South-ampton, and a great distance even from Dover, to which we had got so near.

It had been an hour after midday that we had gained shelter and, whilst coiling down, cooking and changing into shore clothes time passed quickly. A very civil coast watchman boarded us to examine the ship and, although on the morrow duty had to be paid on the gramophone and one or two other little items bought at Riga, we could not help noticing how efficient and courteous were the representatives of our Customs, when compared to the stupid and ill-mannered officials sometimes to be encount-ered in other countries.

It began to rain again and we packed a suitcase, deciding to leave the wet cabin of the ship and sleep ashore for the first time since the cruise had started. It was by then low tide, and we clambered up an iron ladder and made our way shorewards along a somewhat rickety plank. At the ferry we asked whether there was an hotel in the village, and following the directions we crossed the river and went to the " Bell." The comfort of having tea in front of a roaring fire and listening to the patter of rain dashing against the window was too wonderful to describe, and all that skipper and crew could do was to smile inanely at each other. A Sunday paper had room, between the pages devoted to police news, to give a column to describing the violence of the gale. It appeared that the wind had touched forty-eight miles an hour. We were fortunate in having had a powerful ship under us; for we afterwards learnt that the tides meet off Kentish Knock, and we had been caught out in a dangerous corner of the North Sea.

An English inn in an English village made a suitable ending to the cruise, so, as the weather looked unsettled and the wind was likely to remain west, we decided to lay *Annette* up for the winter at Tom Martin's yard. Accordingly we stayed two days at the " Bell," enjoying the comfort of being waited on, and watching our ship being hauled out of her native element to a position in front of the yard. Her gear was stored and our boxes packed, so in two days the time arrived to leave, and so, half sad and half pleased, we took train for the South Coast.

A long cruise in foreign waters is attended by many miseries and by many pleasures, but above all feelings of happiness and hardship there is nothing so strong as the feeling of perfect contentment when all is over and the voyagers are in home port. I suppose we really had received rather more than our share of the rough, and only

CONCLUSION

a few days of the smooth. Having only been able to start so late in the season had been a serious handicap; for on the very day that the cruise commenced the summer ended, and variable headwinds and storms had been the order in August and September. We had been dogged by ill-luck from the start, and on such occasions as the weather had been fine there had been insufficient wind for *Annette*; so that frequently, after gradually wearing out her crew, she was " caught out " before making harbour. Rarely indeed had we been able to leave port without being at least one night at sea, and most of the passages were of much longer duration, so that our light ship's complement of two had very little asleep when at sea.

It must be admitted, however, that Fortune at the last moment smiled on *Annette*, for, when she lay hove-to in the North Sea gale, Dibdin's little cherub alighted and guided her to the Galloper lightship whilst her crew remained below in a state of half-conscious misery. Moreover, the joy of freedom and the ever-changing pleasures of meeting strange people in foreign countries far outbalanced the petty discomforts and the occasional anxieties, so that both skipper and crew now look back on the cruise as a time of great happiness.

A LATVIAN FISHING BOAT

"ANNETTE" HAULED UP AT WALBERSWICK

THE END

APPENDIX

DESCRIPTION OF *ANNETTE II*

*A*NNETTE was a powerful sea-going ketch. Her Thames tonnage was about twelve, but this was due to her exceptional beam of 11 ft. 4 ins., which is such an important figure in the computation of yacht measurement. Her net tonnage would be about six. Her length was 29 ft. 7 ins., and the draft 3 ft. 9 ins., ex centre board—7 ft. 9 ins. with centre board down.

No inside ballast was carried, but outside there was an iron keel of about three and a half tons, which, in view of her excessive beam, proved sufficient to make her extraordinarily stiff. In many ways the yacht was ideal for single-handed sailing, as she was steady on her helm as well as being handy ; moreover her small sail area, distributed according to the ketch rig, made the management of her canvas easy. At the same time this small sail area of 430 feet was in some ways a disadvantage, for it made her slow in normal weather. She took so long to make a passage that there was always a danger of getting caught out before making port. In fact, to make five knots she required half a gale of wind, which, of course, piled up a large sea for so small a ship. During her voyage, almost every individual sail included a night at sea, and on several occasions her crew had to keep at sea for two or three consecutive days without rest.

APPENDIX

Her sails were mainsail, mizzen, storm staysail, balloon staysail and storm trysail. It was found that she was hard headed and exceedingly slow under the storm jib, and consequently in all but the severest weather the balloon staysail was carried. This was almost new and, in spite of much anxiety at times, it never blew away. Her full canvas was about equal to the storm canvas of an average boat of her size, and thus it was rarely necessary to reef. No bowsprit was carried and the end of the mizzen boom was within reach of the deck.

The engine was a 5-h.p. hot bulb engine, but owing to the skipper's ignorance of motors it was hardly used, and the less said about it the better.

As regards the interior. There was one large cabin with two bunks, a table, a writing desk, and ample lockers. Forward was a forecastle with one bunk and storage room for spare sails and gear.

WATCHES

The watches were taken as convenient. The general rule was that the " skipper " took three hours and the " crew " two. But often, to give each other more continuous sleep in long night passages, the skipper took four and the crew three. Sometimes when the skipper was tired the crew took an extra long spell, and correspondingly the skipper stayed at the helm in heavy weather when steering was beyond the strength of the crew.

All deck work to do with the sails, the anchors, and the dinghy fell on the skipper; and all cabin work, such as washing-up and cooking fell on the crew.

APPENDIX

TABLE OF DISTANCES

RIGA to LONDON as "the crow flies," 1000 miles.
Estimated distance sailed, 1350 nautical miles.

*Longest Individual Sails.	Sea miles sailed.	Sea miles direct.	Time. Days.	Hours.	Average speed 3⅓.
Dome Ness (Latvia) to Ljugarn (Gotland). (Helm lashed one night)	160	140	2	1	3⅓
Slesviken (Gotland) to Karlskrona (Sweden). (Helm lashed one night and hove-to six hours)	140	130	3	2	1·9
Skillinge (Sweden) to Copenhagen (Denmark). (Becalmed for three days) . . .	70	70	3	8	0·9
Brunsbüttel (Germany) to Vlieland (Holland). (Becalmed twelve hours) . . .	180	170	2	12	3
YMUIDEN (Holland) to Southwold (England). (Hove-to eight hours) . . .	175	105	2	5	3⅓

* Note delay in every case through calm, gale, or helm lashed to give rest for the crew. This greatly reduced average speed.

RECORD OF ENGINE

Ran six miles. Six engineers to put it in order.
Repair bill, six pounds.

INDEX

INDEX